WORKING WITH VISUAL STUDIO 2019 AND VB.NET

Creating informative RDLC reports from XML

Richard Edwards

WELCOME ABOARD!

Time to dynamically transform computer information into a nice looking reports

Sometimes, beginning a book is hard to do. After all, for some of you reading this, it might appear that using WMI providers and classes to glean information that can then be then transformed into RDLC reports would appear to be a walk in the park.

But then, you have to look at the other side of the glass being half full or half empty and realize that not everybody knows what WMI is much less that there are over 12,000 different classes that can be used.

Beyond that, few know the information can be transformed into element XML or that the DataSet can be used to import the XML and create an xsd file automatically for you.

Of course, there is a reason why the DataSet information is important because that it is what is used to populate the RDLC Report.

However, to get to that end result, we're going to need to build the report using names, column widths and bind the data columns to the field Values that are going to be displayed in the when we tell the ReportViewer to use the DataSet we've created for the report.

The bottom line is, we have a lot to talk about in this book about how to make all of this work together and come out looking like this.

Availability	BytesPerSector	Capabilities	CapabilityDescriptions
	512	3, 4	Random Access, Supports Writing
	512	3, 4	Random Access, Supports Writing
	512	3, 4	Random Access, Supports Writing

On top of that, I'm also going to show you how you can create vertical views that look like this:

PropertyName	PropertyValue
AdminPasswordStatus	3
AutomaticManagedPagefile	TRUE
AutomaticResetBootOption	TRUE
AutomaticResetCapability	TRUE
BootOptionOnLimit	
BootOptionOnWatchDog	
BootROMSupported	TRUE
BootStatus	0, 0, 0, 0, 0, 0, 0, 0, 0, 0
BootupState	Normal boot
Caption	DESKTOP-FU5E0E7
ChassisBootupState	3
ChassisSKUNumber	Default string
CreationClassName	Win32_ComputerSystem
CurrentTimeZone	-420
DaylightInEffect	
Description	AT/AT COMPATIBLE

Is there any documentation on how to create a vertical view?

WHAT YOU WILL LEARN TO DO

The purpose of this book is to explain at every step of the way how to go from a list of WMI Namespaces, categories, and classes to a dynamically created rdlc report using Visual Studio 2019.

You will learn how to convert the properties of the selected WMI Class into XML, how to format the information so that both horizontal and vertical views can be created, why a DataGridView is used to automatically adjust the field widths for you and what needs to be done with the rdlc file so that the entire process not only works but can produce over 450 reports – perfectly aligned and usable within minutes after reading this book.

The best part of reading this book is the fact that you will be able to automate the updates to the predefined rdlc files without having to redo each report every time the information changes.

We've got a lot to cover and I'm excited. So let's to get started.

IT ALL STARTS WITH SOME WMI BASICS

Creating a user interface using VB.Net and the COM version: WbemScripting

There are a lot of awesome books on WMI, providers and classes. You have Winmgmts or WbemScripting.SWbemLocator to connect both locally and remotely, you can add the DCOM – Distributed Component Object Model – Authentication and Impersonation permissions, you can decide to use an asynchronous or synchronous connections and have seven ways to make all of this work.

WORKING WITH LOCAL AND SYNCHRONOUS CONNECTIONS

For right now, our primary concern is with creating a connection locally and retrieving all of the namespaces and classes each namespace has as collection of providers and classes.

Because we are connecting locally, we can use either one of these methods:

```
Dim svc as Object = GetObject("winmgmts:\\.\root\CIMV2")
Or:
Dim loc as Object = CreateObject("WbemScripting.SWbemLocator")
Dim svc as Object = loc.ConnectServer(".", "root\CIMV2")
```

Because we are using a local connection, username and password is not required. In fact, even if you tried using a username and password – which can only be used with the SWbemLocator:

Dim svc as Object = loc.ConnectServer(".", "root\CIMV2", username, password)

The code when run would generate an error telling you, essentially, that username and password is not required when creating a local connection.

SECURITY

It has honestly been 20 years since I supported DCOM connectivity issues. So, please forgive me if I sound a bit rusty here.

Go to the start icon on the taskbar, right click on it, select run, type in dcomcnfg and press enter. This screen will popup:

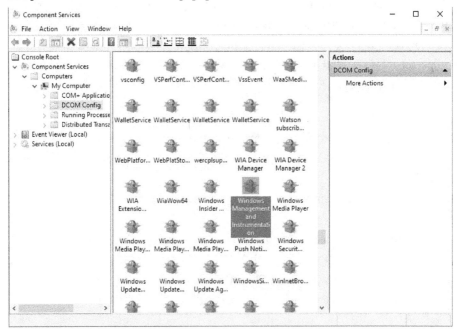

Expand Component Services, Computers and My Computer. Click on DCOM Config.

You might get an error message telling you that a particular ClassID wasn't properly registered. Click ok. When all the icons show up in the middle of the window as shown above, look for Windows Management and Instrumentation.

Right click on the ICON and choose properties. Another window will show up looking like this:

Don't change anything as if you don't know what you are doing, you could cause an issue where you would either be calling technical support or rebuilding your machine.

What you are looking at is the permissions for winmgmt. WbemScripting.SWbemLocator has its own AppID or Application Identifier. And is listed separately.

But the one thing you will notice is the Authentication Level is set to Default. That means the setting is, by default already set for you. Also meaning, since you are connecting locally that the local service is running at the default level which also happens to be PktPrivacy and has a numerical value of 6. There are seven of these.

WbemAuthenticationLevelDefault	**= 0**
WbemAuthenticationLevelNone	**= 1**
WbemAuthenticationLevelConnect	**= 2**
WbemAuthenticationLevelCall	**= 3**
WbemAuthenticationLevelPkt	**= 4**
WbemAuthenticationLevelPktIntegrity	**= 5**
WbemAuthenticationLevelPktPrivacy	**= 6**

When you see Default in the properties window of Windows Management and Instrumentation it means use the default settings. Meaning not adding:

svc.Security_.AuthenticationLevel = 6 'Packet Privacy

Also means use the default setting which is the same thing by default.
When you select something other than the default impersonation level:

svc.Security_.ImpersonationLevel = 3 'Impersonate

There was a time when these impersonationLevel settings required some work to get them right and things like Identify meant you had to have the right username and password added to the Identity tab and only that person would be trusted to connect to the machine.

The problem with that is winmgmt doesn't have the ability to pass in a username or password. In fact, winmgmt's use is usually based on Domain Administrator's credentials enabling the Domain Administrator to connect and glean information from joined domain machines without having to pass username and password.

If you look at all the examples of using winmgmt, you will see:

```
winmgmts:{impersonationLevel=Impersonate}!\\
```
or:

```
winmgmts:{impersonationLevel=impersonate,
authenticationLevel=PktPrivacy}!\\
```

Which, if you really want to get technical, is a total and complete waste of time typing them in since they are the defaults. Below are the various values you can try using on your local or remote connections. Just remember that on most modern OSes, the default values already setup will work just fine for both remote and local connections.

wbemImpersonationLevelAnonymous	=1
wbemImpersonationLevelIdentify	=2
wbemImpersonationLevelImpersonate	=3
wbemImpersonationLevelDelegate	=4

WHAT WBEM MEANS AND HOW IT WORKS

WBEM stands for Web Based Enterprise Management. Yep, it is old school....like dinosaur old school. Back in the old days when the term heavy client was the front end for most web based applications, all you had to do is connect and ask for information about a specific machine.

Unfortunately, that information wasn't very secure, and, while you could glean information from both local and remote machines inside a web page, a mechanism was needed to make the entire process locked down and secured.

Unlike the internal winmgmt service for Administrators – which also used DCOM – WBEMScripting and DCOM worked well together.

Only problem was it also opened up a whole bunch of security issues. Which is why most admins have locked down or completely disabled WMI as a way to glean information from remote machines using the internet.

But the Intranet is a completely different bread of cat. Internal networks live behind firewalls or are totally internal systems. Which is why things like System Center Operations Manager (SCOM) can work at all.

However, for smaller business infrastructures that having the money or the desire to purchase SCOM either depend on WBEMScripting or something like Simple Network Management Protocol (SNMP) that uses management information base (MIBs) numerical requests to gather the information from bork local and remote machines.

AND NOW

On your local machine and on a fresh install without any additional software added, there are close to 12,000 different classes that you can call using the right namespace and classname combinations.

The most popular namespace is root\cimv2. On my machine with a lot of software installed, there are over 1,200 classes that can be called upon and can be grouped into seven basic categories: Hardware classes, eventlog classes, performance counter classes, registry classes, software classes, system classes, and security classes.

GETTING STARTED

While all of this is like having a gold mine of information available to you on your local machine, it does take around 45 seconds initially to connect using DCOM and, depending on the number of namespaces available, it could take a few minutes before all of them show up in the namespaces ToolstripCombobox1 collection.

With that said, I created a simple Windows forms project with a MDIParent form being part of the mix and responsible for parenting the first form as shown below. I have no intention on using the menu or the toolstrip. But since they were there, I just left them.

I then clicked on the project in the solution explorer and set the MDIParent form as the startup form.

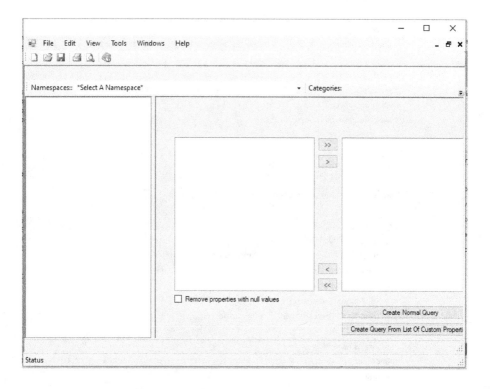

The code in the MDIParent1_load is as follows:

```
Private Sub MDIParent1_Load(sender As Object, e As EventArgs) Handles MyBase.Load

    Me.WindowState = FormWindowState.Maximized
    Application.DoEvents()

    Dim myform As New Form1
    myform.MdiParent = Me
    myform.WindowState = FormWindowState.Maximized
    myform.Show()

End Sub
```

This gets everything started. The Form1_load code looks like this:

```vb
Imports WbemScripting
Public Class Form1

    Dim max As Integer = 0
    Private Sub Form1_Load(sender As Object, e As EventArgs) Handles MyBase.Load

        ToolStripComboBox1.Items.Add("*Select A Namespace*")
        ToolStripComboBox1.Text = "*Select A Namespace*"
        EnumNamespaces("root")
        ToolStripComboBox1.Sorted = True

    End Sub
    Public Sub EnumNamespaces(ByVal tstr As String)

        ToolStripComboBox1.Items.Add(tstr)

        Try
            Dim loc As New SWbemLocator
            Dim svc As SWbemServices = loc.ConnectServer(".", tstr)
            Dim objs As SWbemObjectSet = svc.InstancesOf("__Namespace")
            For Each obj In objs
                Application.DoEvents()
                EnumNamespaces(tstr & "\" & obj.Name)
            Next
        Catch ex As Exception
            Err.Clear()
            Exit Sub
        End Try

    End Sub
```

This code works because I added a COM reference to the Microsoft WMI Scripting V1.2 Library to the project:

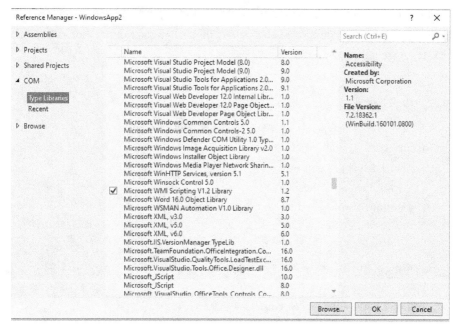

and then included it using the imports statement above the Public Class Form1 statement at the very top of the form code:

```
Imports WbemScripting
Public Class Form1
```

I have learned through the school of hard knocks that sorting should not be enabled when enumerating through a large number of items that need to be sorted. I is better to wait until the enumeration process is done.

That is why Sorted = true is called after the enumeration routine is finished and not while it is running through the possible namespaces:

```
ToolStripComboBox1.Items.Add("*Select A Namespace*")
ToolStripComboBox1.Text = "*Select A Namespace*"
EnumNamespaces("root")
ToolStripComboBox1.Sorted = True
```

The enumeration routine is pretty much cut and dry. There is a try catch routine involved because the namespace being passed in through the enumeration sub routine tries to create namespaces that don't exist.

```
Dim svc As SWbemServices = loc.ConnectServer(".", tstr)
        Dim         objs        As          SWbemObjectSet         =
svc.InstancesOf("__Namespace")
        For Each obj In objs
            Application.DoEvents()
            EnumNamespaces(tstr & "\" & obj.Name)
        Next
```

This error occurs here:

```
Dim objs As SWbemObjectSet = svc.InstancesOf("__Namespace")
```

It occurs on the above line because when there are no more additional namespaces to be found, it errors. The Try Catch routine traps for the error and stops trying to run the routine by exiting sub.

Anyway, once populated, you can then choose a specific namespace and discover what classes are part of that specific namespace.

I've added a custom routine that I've used over the years that makes sense. There are, basically three different types of classes. Those that are SuperClasses, Classes without underscores which signify that they are not part of any category and category Classes that have underscores like Win32__.

```
Private Sub ToolStripComboBox1_SelectedIndexChanged(sender As Object, e As EventArgs) Handles
ToolStripComboBox1.SelectedIndexChanged

   If ToolStripComboBox1.Text <> "*Select A Namespace*" Then

       ToolStripComboBox2.Items.Clear()
       ToolStripComboBox2.Items.Add("*Select A Category*")
       ToolStripComboBox2.Text = "*Select A Category*"
```

```
Dim pos As Integer = 0
Dim odic As Object = CreateObject("Scripting.Dictionary")
ComboBox1.Items.Clear()
Dim svc As SWbemServices = loc.ConnectServer(".", ToolStripComboBox1.Text)
Dim objs As SWbemObjectSet = svc.SubclassesOf()
For Each obj As Object In objs

    pos = InStr(obj.Path_.Class, "_")

    Select Case pos

        Case 0

            If odic.Exists(obj.Path_.Class) = False Then
                ComboBox1.Items.Add(obj.Path_.Class)
                odic.Add(obj.Path_.Class, obj.Path_.Class)
            End If

        Case 1

            If odic.Exists("SuperClasses") = False Then
                ComboBox1.Items.Add("SuperClasses")
                odic.Add("SuperClasses", "SuperClasses")
            End If

        Case > 1

            If odic.Exists(Mid(obj.Path_.Class, 1, pos - 1)) = False Then
                ComboBox1.Items.Add(Mid(obj.Path_.Class, 1, pos - 1))
                odic.Add(Mid(obj.Path_.Class, 1, pos - 1), Mid(obj.Path_.Class, 1, pos - 1))
            End If

    End Select


Next

For x As Integer = 0 To ComboBox1.Items.Count - 1
    ToolStripComboBox2.Items.Add(ComboBox1.Items(x).ToString())
Next

End If

End Sub
```

At this point in the program, we now have list of namespaces, selected one and are now waiting for the categories to show up in the categories ToolstripComboBox2.

The only real curveball thrown into this piece of logic is the fact that I used a hidden combobox to gather all the items I found that would be used to populate the ToolstripComboBox2.

I'm about to use it again since the Treeview control does a lousy job of sorting.

Also, notice that I used the COM version of the dictionary object to assure that only one entry in each category is added to the combobox.

Here's my concern with all of this. If it takes so much time to create a list of namespaces and it is on your machine, why not create a script and create a text file that includes all the current namespaces?

Well the answer is you certainly could as long as you know the list isn't going to change and, in truth, you could simply use the script below to do it. But it is still going to take the same amount of time to create the categories as it would take to do the namespaces.

```
Dim fso
Dim ws
Dim txtstream
Dim odic
Dim l
Dim s


Set ws = createobject("Wscript.Shell")
Set fso = CreateObject("Scripting.FilesystemObject")
Set txtstream = fso.OpenTextFile(ws.currentDirectory & "\Namespaces.txt", 2, true, -2)
Set odic = CreateObject("Scripting.Dictionary")
EnumNamespaces("root")
txtstream.Close

Sub EnumNamespaces(ByVal nspace)

If odic.Exists(nspace) = false then
 txtstream.WriteLine(nspace)
 odic.Add nspace, nspace
End If
```

```
On error Resume Next

Set objs = GetObject("Winmgmts:\\.\" & nspace).InstancesOf("___Namespace", &H20000)

If err.Number <> 0 Then
  err.Clear
  Exit Sub
End If

For each obj in objs
  EnumNamespaces(nspace & "\" & obj.Name)
Next

End Sub
```

That will create a list of namespaces that can be open in notepad and then copy and pasted into the namespaces toolstripComboBox1.Items property window. But you will still be waiting on the next ToolStripComboBox items to appear since you still have to connect through DCOM.

With that said, here's the code that populates the Treeview with the classes in the selected category:

```
Private Sub ToolStripComboBox2_SelectedIndexChanged(sender As Object, e As EventArgs) Handles
ToolStripComboBox2.SelectedIndexChanged

If ToolStripComboBox2.Text <> "*Select A Category*" Then
  TreeView1.Nodes.Clear()

  Dim pos As Integer = 0
  ComboBox1.Items.Clear()
  Dim svc As SWbemServices = loc.ConnectServer(".", ToolStripComboBox1.Text)
  Dim objs As SWbemObjectSet = svc.SubclassesOf()
  For Each obj As Object In objs

    pos = InStr(obj.Path_.Class, "_")

    Select Case pos

    Case 0

      If obj.Path_.Class = ToolStripComboBox2.Text Then
        ComboBox1.Items.Add(obj.Path_.Class)
```

```
            End If

        Case 1

            If ToolStripComboBox2.Text = "SuperClasses" Then
                ComboBox1.Items.Add(obj.Path_.Class)
            End If

        Case > 1

            If Mid(obj.Path_.Class, 1, pos - 1) = ToolStripComboBox2.Text Then
                ComboBox1.Items.Add(obj.Path_.Class)
            End If

        End Select


    Next

    Dim tn As TreeNode = Nothing

    If ComboBox1.Items.Count > 0 Then
        tn = TreeView1.Nodes.Add("Classes")
    End If
    For x As Integer = 0 To ComboBox1.Items.Count - 1
        tn.Nodes.Add(ComboBox1.Items(x).ToString())
    Next

    End If


End Sub
```

At this point you should be able to see the next page list of selected classes. Notice that a single TreeNode was created so that the Treeview code would not run unless the selected node was level one.

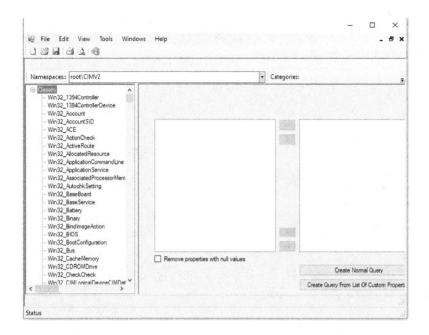

After you've selected a class, the code under the Treeview is run so that the selected class is provides you with a list of properties that class exposes. These properties are what you will be using to create the Element XML file, the schema xsd file and the rdlc report from.

```
Private Sub TreeView1_AfterSelect(sender As Object, e As TreeViewEventArgs) Handles TreeView1.AfterSelect


    ListBox1.Items.Clear()
    ListBox2.Items.Clear()

    Button1.Enabled = False
    Button2.Enabled = False
    Button3.Enabled = False
    Button4.Enabled = False
    Button5.Enabled = False
    Button6.Enabled = False


    If TreeView1.SelectedNode.Level = 1 Then
```

```
Dim svc As SWbemServices = loc.ConnectServer(".", ToolStripComboBox1.Text)
Dim obj As SWbemObject = svc.Get(TreeView1.SelectedNode.Text)
max = obj.Properties_.Count - 1
For Each prop As Object In obj.Properties_
    ListBox1.Items.Add(prop.Name)
Next

Button1.Enabled = True
Button2.Enabled = True
Button3.Enabled = False
Button4.Enabled = False
Button5.Enabled = False
Button6.Enabled = False

End If

End Sub
```

That gets you to here:

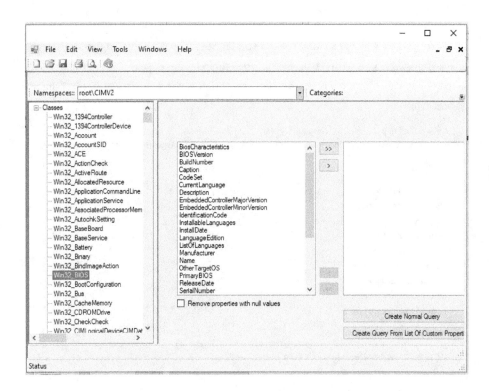

A QUICK GUIDE TO THE THREE METHODS USED TO WORK WITH THE PROPERY DATA

Both Get and InstancesOf methods from the SWbemServices class will enable us to view all the objects and PropertyData information using the standard routines below.

```
Dim ob as SWbemObject = svc.Get("Win32_BIOS")
For each SWbemObject in ob.Instances_
    For each prop as SWbemProperty in obj.Properties_

    Next
Next
```

```
Dim objs as SWbemObjectSet = svc.InstancesOf("Win32_BIOS")
For each SWbemObject in objs
    For each prop as SWbemProperty in obj.Properties_

    Next
Next
```

But the one that will enable us to create a custom query is ExecQuery:

```
Dim objs as SWbemObjectSet = svc.ExecQuery("Select * From Win32_BIOS")
For each SWbemObject in objs
    For each prop as SWbemProperty in obj.Properties_

    Next
Next
```

The routine above will be used when the list of property names. The reason why I am mentioning this here is because the code under the TreeView1_AfterSelect event set the stage to decide whether or not we should be using a custom query or not.

```vb
Private Sub TreeView1_AfterSelect(sender As Object, e As TreeViewEventArgs) Handles TreeView1.AfterSelect


        ListBox1.Items.Clear()
        ListBox2.Items.Clear()

        Button1.Enabled = False
        Button2.Enabled = False
        Button3.Enabled = False
        Button4.Enabled = False
        Button5.Enabled = False
        Button6.Enabled = False


        If TreeView1.SelectedNode.Level = 1 Then

            Dim svc As SWbemServices = loc.ConnectServer(".", ToolStripComboBox1.Text)
            Dim obj As SWbemObject = svc.Get(TreeView1.SelectedNode.Text)
            For Each prop As Object In obj.Properties_
                ListBox1.Items.Add(prop.Name)
            Next

            Button1.Enabled = True
            Button2.Enabled = True
            Button3.Enabled = False
            Button4.Enabled = False
            Button5.Enabled = False
            Button6.Enabled = False

        End If

    End Sub
```

HOW THE LISTBOXES ARE MANAGED

Each button has a specific purpose. The buttons between the two ListBoxes manage how many items are moved from left to right and from right to left. The first top button pushes everything over to the right. The second only a selected item. The Third removes only the selected item from the collection of custom properties to be used when a custom query should be created. The fourth removes all of the items from the right listbox and then clears and fills the left listbox with the WMI class properties.

Button5 moves a selected item in the right listbox up one and button 6 moves a selected item down one.

In all cases where the selected item needs to be moved, it has to be selected otherwise the routine exits as it has nothing to do.

The primary purpose of the first ListBox is to provide a list of properties that could be selected – added to the second list and removed from the first. The code to do that is as follows:

```
Private Sub Button1_Click(sender As Object, e As EventArgs) Handles Button1.Click

    If max = ListBox1.Items.Count Then

        ListBox2.Items.AddRange(ListBox1.Items)
        ListBox1.Items.Clear()
        Button1.Enabled = False
        Button2.Enabled = False
        Button3.Enabled = True
        Button4.Enabled = True
        Button5.Enabled = True
        Button6.Enabled = True

    Else

        ListBox1.Items.Clear()
        ListBox2.Items.Clear()

        Dim svc As SWbemServices = loc.ConnectServer(".", ToolStripComboBox1.Text)
        Dim obj As SWbemObject = svc.Get(TreeView1.SelectedNode.Text)
        max = obj.Properties_.Count - 1
        For Each prop As Object In obj.Properties_
            ListBox2.Items.Add(prop.Name)
        Next

        Button1.Enabled = False
        Button2.Enabled = False
        Button3.Enabled = True
        Button4.Enabled = True
        Button5.Enabled = True
        Button6.Enabled = True


    End If

    End Sub
```

Below is the code for button2:

```
Private Sub Button2_Click(sender As Object, e As EventArgs) Handles Button2.Click

    If ListBox1.Text <> "" Then
        ListBox2.Items.Add(ListBox1.Text)
        ListBox1.Items.Remove(ListBox1.Text)

        Select Case ListBox2.Items.Count

            Case 0

                Button3.Enabled = False
                Button4.Enabled = False
                Button5.Enabled = False
                Button6.Enabled = False

            Case 1

                Button3.Enabled = True
                Button4.Enabled = False
                Button5.Enabled = False
                Button6.Enabled = False

            Case > 1

                Button3.Enabled = True
                Button4.Enabled = True
                Button5.Enabled = True
                Button6.Enabled = True

        End Select

        Select Case ListBox1.Items.Count

            Case 0

                Button1.Enabled = False
                Button2.Enabled = False

            Case 1

                Button1.Enabled = False
                Button2.Enabled = True
```

```
                Case > 1

                    Button1.Enabled = True
                    Button2.Enabled = True

            End Select

        End If

    End Sub
```

Below is the code for button3:

```
    Private Sub Button3_Click(sender As Object, e As EventArgs) Handles Button3.Click

        If ListBox2.Text <> "" Then

            ListBox2.Items.Remove(ListBox2.Text)

            Select Case ListBox2.Items.Count

                Case 0

                    ListBox1.Items.Clear()
                    ListBox2.Items.Clear()

                    Dim      obj      As      Object      =      GetObject("Winmgmts:\\.\"      &
        ToolStripComboBox1.Text).Get(TreeView1.SelectedNode.Text)
                    For Each prop As Object In obj.Properties_
                        ListBox1.Items.Add(prop.Name)
                    Next

                    Button1.Enabled = True
                    Button2.Enabled = True
                    Button3.Enabled = False
                    Button4.Enabled = False

                Case 1

                    Button3.Enabled = True
                    Button4.Enabled = False
                    Button5.Enabled = False
```

```
                    Button6.Enabled = False

            Case > 1

                    Button3.Enabled = True
                    Button4.Enabled = True
                    Button5.Enabled = True
                    Button6.Enabled = True

        End Select

        Select Case ListBox1.Items.Count

            Case 0

                    Button1.Enabled = False
                    Button2.Enabled = False

            Case 1

                    Button1.Enabled = False
                    Button2.Enabled = True

            Case > 1

                    Button1.Enabled = True
                    Button2.Enabled = True

        End Select

        End If

    End Sub
```

Below is the code for button4:

```
    Private Sub Button4_Click(sender As Object, e As EventArgs) Handles Button4.Click
        ListBox1.Items.Clear()
        ListBox2.Items.Clear()

        Dim      obj      As      Object      =      GetObject("Winmgmts:\\.\"      &
    ToolStripComboBox1.Text).Get(TreeView1.SelectedNode.Text)
        For Each prop As Object In obj.Properties_
```

```
        ListBox1.Items.Add(prop.Name)
    Next

    Button1.Enabled = True
    Button2.Enabled = True
    Button3.Enabled = False
    Button4.Enabled = False
    Button5.Enabled = False
    Button6.Enabled = False

End Sub
```

Below is the code for Button5:

```
Private Sub Button5_Click(sender As Object, e As EventArgs) Handles Button5.Click

    If ListBox2.Text = "" Then Exit Sub
    If ListBox2.SelectedIndex > 0 Then
        Dim up As String = ListBox2.Items(ListBox2.SelectedIndex)
        Dim dn As String = ListBox2.Items(ListBox2.SelectedIndex - 1)
        ListBox2.Items(ListBox2.SelectedIndex - 1) = up
        ListBox2.Items(ListBox2.SelectedIndex) = dn
    End If

End Sub
```

Below is the code for Button6:

```
Private Sub Button6_Click(sender As Object, e As EventArgs) Handles Button6.Click

    If ListBox2.Text = "" Then Exit Sub
    If ListBox2.SelectedIndex < ListBox2.Items.Count - 1 Then
        Dim up As String = ListBox2.Items(ListBox2.SelectedIndex)
        Dim dn As String = ListBox2.Items(ListBox2.SelectedIndex + 1)
        ListBox2.Items(ListBox2.SelectedIndex + 1) = up
        ListBox2.Items(ListBox2.SelectedIndex) = dn
    End If

End Sub
```

As you can see from the above two routines, the text value must have a value otherwise the routine exists. Of course the same thing can be said for the single item to the left and the single item to the right.

The other condition which must be met for each of the up and down routines is that in the case of the up routine, the SelectedIndex is not 0 and in the case of the down routine, the SelectedIndex is not equal to the Items count-1.

Obviously, you can't move the top most item up one nor can you move the bottom item down one either.

The other pieces of logic involving the movement of items from the left to right are:

Is there more than two items in the right listbox? If yes, then enable Button6 and Button6. If no, disable them.

Is there any items in the left listbox? If yes, then don't disable button1 or button2. If no, then disable button1 and button2.

The same checks are made for the removal of items in listbox2.

Is there more than two items in the right listbox? If yes, then enable Button6 and Button6. If no, disable them.

Are there any items in the left listbox2 If yes, then don't disable button3 or button4. If not then disable button3, button4, button5, button6, clear both ListBoxes, repopulate Listbox1 and enable Button1 and Button2.

If the count is 1 then enable button3 and button4. Disable button5 and button6.

If the count is greater than 1 then enable button3, button4, button5 and button6.

THIS IS WHERE IT GETS REALLY INTERESTING

If you have worked with WMI and with the property collections, you know that there are a lot of times when those properties come back with nothing at all. So, you effectively have empty spaces between information making the report hard to read and looking like a mouth missing a few teeth when someone smiles.

At first, you might think, well, if I sample the first row of columns, I will know which ones come back with information and the ones that don't. I could just remove the ones that don't, and the report will look like solid information. For the most part that would be a correct assumption until you do a report on Win32_Process where the Command line doesn't supply a value for quite a while until a physical file is used.

That's where this routine comes into play:

```vbnet
Private Sub CheckBox1_CheckedChanged(sender As Object, e As EventArgs) Handles
CheckBox1.CheckedChanged

    If classname = "" Then Exit Sub

    If CheckBox1.Checked = True Then


        ListBox1.Items.Clear()
        ListBox2.Items.Clear()

        Button1.Enabled = False
        Button2.Enabled = False
        Button3.Enabled = False
        Button4.Enabled = False
        Button5.Enabled = False
        Button6.Enabled = False

        Dim odic As Object = CreateObject("Scripting.Dictionary")

        If TreeView1.SelectedNode.Level = 1 Then

            Dim ob As SWbemObject = GetObject("Winmgmts:\\.\" &
ToolStripComboBox1.Text).Get(TreeView1.SelectedNode.Text, &H20000)
            Dim prop As Object

            For Each obj In ob.Instances_
                For Each prop In obj.Properties_
                    If IsDBNull(prop.Value) = False Then
                        If odic.Exists(prop.Name) = False Then
                            odic.Add(prop.Name, prop.Name)
                        End If
                    End If
                Next
            Next

            Dim keys As Object = odic.Keys

            For x As Integer = 0 To UBound(keys) - 1
                ListBox2.Items.Add(keys(x))
            Next
```

```
                    Button1.Enabled = False
                    Button2.Enabled = False
                    Button3.Enabled = True
                    Button4.Enabled = False
                    Button5.Enabled = True
                    Button6.Enabled = True
                    Button7.Enabled = False
                    Button8.Enabled = True


                End If



            Else



                ListBox1.Items.Clear()
                ListBox2.Items.Clear()

                Button1.Enabled = False
                Button2.Enabled = False
                Button3.Enabled = False
                Button4.Enabled = False
                Button5.Enabled = False
                Button6.Enabled = False


                If TreeView1.SelectedNode.Level = 1 Then

                    Dim      obj      As      Object      =      GetObject("Winmgmts:\\.\"      &
                ToolStripComboBox1.Text).Get(TreeView1.SelectedNode.Text)
                    max = obj.Properties_.Count - 1
                    For Each prop As Object In obj.Properties_
                        ListBox1.Items.Add(prop.Name)
                    Next

                    Button1.Enabled = True
                    Button2.Enabled = True
                    Button3.Enabled = False
                    Button4.Enabled = False
                    Button5.Enabled = False
                    Button6.Enabled = False
                    Button7.Enabled = True
```

```
            Button8.Enabled = True

        End If

    End If

End Sub
```

The magic happens here:

```
For Each obj In ob.Instances_
    For Each prop In obj.Properties_
        If IsDBNull(prop.Value) = False Then
            If odic.Exists(prop.Name) = False Then
                odic.Add(prop.Name, prop.Name)
            End If
        End If
    Next
Next
```

Basically, the routine is saying, while I can normally expect to find null values at the very beginning of the collections of rows and properties at the very first row of entries, I'm going to go through all of them just in case somewhere along the way one or more comes back with some information.

So the routine uses a dictionary object and adds to it a property value that isn't null and does this just once. When done, only those properties that do return information will be part of the collection.

The Create Normal Query Button7 is never disabled because it looks for an assigned Classname value and you won't have one until you select one from the list of class names from the list of classnames displayed in the Treeview.

```
Private Sub Button7_Click(sender As Object, e As EventArgs) Handles Button7.Click

    If classname = "" Then Exit Sub

    Dim myform As New Form2
    myform.MdiParent = Me.MdiParent
    myform.WindowState = FormWindowState.Maximized
```

```
    myform.Visible = True


    Dim ds As New System.Data.DataSet

    Dim myform1 As New Form5
    myform1.MdiParent = Me.MdiParent
    myform1.ReportViewer1.LocalReport.ReportPath = Application.StartupPath & "\" & classname & ".rdlc"
    myform1.ReportViewer1.LocalReport.DataSources.Clear()
    ds.ReadXml(Application.StartupPath & "\" & classname & ".xml")
    myform1.ReportViewer1.LocalReport.DataSources.Add(New
Microsoft.Reporting.WinForms.ReportDataSource("DataSet1", ds.Tables(0)))
    myform1.ReportViewer1.RefreshReport()
    myform1.Show()

End Sub
```

The Create Query From List Of Custom Properties Button6 is disabled at design time because unless you've cleaned the fields or only selected a subset of the property names, you're just doing the same thing as a regular query.

```
Private Sub Button8_Click(sender As Object, e As EventArgs) Handles Button8.Click

    If classname = "" Then Exit Sub
    If ListBox2.Items.Count = 0 Then
        querystring = "Select * from " & classname
    End If
    If ListBox2.Items.Count > 0 Then
        querystring = "Select "
        Dim tempstr As String = ""
        For x As Integer = 0 To ListBox2.Items.Count - 1
            If tempstr <> "" Then
                tempstr = tempstr & ", "
            End If
            tempstr = tempstr & ListBox2.Items(x)
        Next
        querystring = querystring & tempstr & " from " & classname
    End If

    Dim myform As New Form6
    myform.MdiParent = Me.MdiParent
    myform.Show()
```

End Sub

WHAT JUST HAPPENED

All of this is well and good and will work....except here.

Take a look at the query:

Select AcceptPause, AcceptStop, Caption, CheckPoint, CreationClassName, DelayedAutoStart, DesktopInteract, DisplayName, ErrorControl, ExitCode, Name, PathName, ProcessId, ServiceSpecificExitCode, ServiceType, Started, StartMode, StartName, State, Status, SystemCreationClassName, SystemName, TagId, WaitHint, Description, DisconnectedSessions from Win32_Service

There is nothing wrong with that query and it would normally work correctly.

Below is the usual Win32_Service entry:

```
instance of Win32_Service
{
            AcceptPause = FALSE;
            AcceptStop = FALSE;
```

```
        Caption = "Telephony";
        CheckPoint = 0;
        CreationClassName = "Win32_Service";
        DelayedAutoStart = FALSE;
        Description = "Provides Telephony API (TAPI) support for programs that control
telephony devices on the local computer and, through the LAN, on servers that are also running the
service.";
        DesktopInteract = FALSE;
        DisplayName = "Telephony";
        ErrorControl = "Normal";
        ExitCode = 1077;
        Name = "TapiSrv";
        PathName = "C:\\Windows\\System32\\svchost.exe -k NetworkService -p";
        ProcessId = 0;
        ServiceSpecificExitCode = 0;
        ServiceType = "Share Process";
        Started = FALSE;
        StartMode = "Manual";
        StartName = "NT AUTHORITY\\NetworkService";
        State = "Stopped";
        Status = "OK";
        SystemCreationClassName = "Win32_ComputerSystem";
        SystemName = "DESKTOP-FU5E0E7";
        TagId = 0;
        WaitHint = 0;
};
```

But right after this one, you will see why:

```
instance of Win32_TerminalService
{
        AcceptPause = FALSE;
        AcceptStop = TRUE;
        Caption = "Remote Desktop Services";
        CheckPoint = 0;
        CreationClassName = "Win32_Service";
        DelayedAutoStart = FALSE;
        Description = "Allows users to connect interactively to a remote computer. Remote
Desktop and Remote Desktop Session Host Server depend on this service.  To prevent remote use of
this computer, clear the checkboxes on the Remote tab of the System properties control panel item.";
        DesktopInteract = FALSE;
        DisconnectedSessions = 1;
        DisplayName = "Remote Desktop Services";
```

```
    ErrorControl = "Normal";
    ExitCode = 0;
    Name = "TermService";
    PathName = "C:\\Windows\\System32\\svchost.exe -k NetworkService";
    ProcessId = 1644;
    ServiceSpecificExitCode = 0;
    ServiceType = "Share Process";
    Started = TRUE;
    StartMode = "Manual";
    StartName = "NT Authority\\NetworkService";
    State = "Running";
    Status = "OK";
    SystemCreationClassName = "Win32_ComputerSystem";
    SystemName = "DESKTOP-FU5E0E7";
    TagId = 0;
    TotalSessions = 2;
    WaitHint = 0;
};
```

Apparently either the powers to be at Microsoft thought this entry just had to be part of the Win32_Service entries and didn't bother to even change the name of the entry to Win32_Service (plus two additional properties) or they forgot that there is an entire sub-directory:

root\CIMV2\TerminalServices

For such entries.

There are 28 fields in the TerminalServices entry but only 26 in the standard Win32_Service entries.

Obviously, this entry is in the wrong place and will cause issues not only for queries but for dealing with its existence in the collection of rows and columns inside the provider itself.

So, how do we get around it – since it hasn't been fixed in over 3 versions of OSes? Here's the additional code needed to do it:

```vbnet
Dim x As Integer = 0
If classname = "Win32_Service" Then

    Namesdic = New System.Collections.Generic.Dictionary(Of Integer, String)
    Widthdic = New System.Collections.Generic.Dictionary(Of Integer, String)

    Dim props As Object = GetObject("Winmgmts:\\.\root\cimv2").Get("Win32_Service").Properties_
    For Each prop As Object In props
        Namesdic.Add(x, prop.Name)
        x = x + 1
    Next

    Dim ds1 As New System.Data.DataSet
    Dim dt As New System.Data.DataTable
    ds1.Tables.Add(dt)

    For Each prop As Object In props
        ds1.Tables(0).Columns.Add(prop.Name)
    Next
    Dim objs As Object = GetObject("Winmgmts:\\.\root\cimv2").InstancesOf("Win32_Service")
    For Each obj In objs
        Dim dr As System.Data.DataRow = ds1.Tables(0).NewRow()
        For Each prop As Object In props
            dr.Item(prop.Name) = GetValue(prop.Name, obj)
        Next
        ds1.Tables(0).Rows.Add(dr)
    Next

    Dim myform2 As New Form7
    myform2.DataGridView1.DataSource = ds1.Tables(0)

    myform2.MdiParent = Me.MdiParent
    myform2.WindowState = FormWindowState.Maximized
    myform2.Visible = True

    ds1.WriteXml(Application.StartupPath & "\Win32_Service.xml")
    ds1.WriteXmlSchema(Application.StartupPath & "\Win32_Service.xsd")

    Dim y As Integer = 0

    myform2.DataGridView1.AutoSizeColumnsMode = DataGridViewAutoSizeColumnMode.AllCells
    For y = 0 To myform2.DataGridView1.Columns.Count - 1
        Dim d As Double = (myform2.DataGridView1.Rows(0).Cells(y).Size.Width / 90)
```

```
        Widthdic.Add(y, d.ToString())
      Next

      Myform2.Close()

      Module1.Create_The_Report("Win32_Service")

      Dim myform3 As New Form5
      myform3.MdiParent = Me.MdiParent
      myform3.ReportViewer1.LocalReport.ReportPath = Application.StartupPath & "\Win32_Service.rdlc"
      myform3.ReportViewer1.LocalReport.DataSources.Clear()
      Dim ds2 As New System.Data.DataSet
      ds2.ReadXml(Application.StartupPath & "\Win32_Service.xml")
      myform3.ReportViewer1.LocalReport.DataSources.Add(New
Microsoft.Reporting.WinForms.ReportDataSource("DataSet1", ds2.Tables(0)))
      myform3.ReportViewer1.RefreshReport()
      myform3.Show()

      Exit Sub
    End If
```

WHAT IS GOING ON HERE

This code is pretty simple. First, I have two forms. One with a blank DataGridView control on it and the other with a completely empty Report Viewer control on it.

The first step is to create a new names dictionary and new numerical dictionary.

The second step is to populate the names dictionary with all the properties that the provider normally supports. I do this by using get as the provider was designed to work with 26 properties and not 28.

The third step is to create a collection of those 26 property names that even the Win32_TerminalService supports and not include the extra two.

The fourth step is to create a DataSet and a DataTable and add the new DataTable to the DataSet.

The fifth step is to add the Columns to the DataSet.DataTable(0).Columns.

The sixth step is to add the values for each row of properties in the collection. Once the data has been added to the dataset, the next step is to create an instance of the form with the empty DataGridView and populate it by binding the DataGridView1.Datasource to the Dataset.

I also make the xml and xsd files.

Next, the DataGridView1.AutoSizeColumnMode and set it to GridViewAutoSizeColumnMode.AllCells.

After this is set, I create the numerical collection of the decimal values for each cell size width and divide it by a value that works with the font size of the report's field width.

I then close the from with the DataGridView on it and tell the module I want to create the report.

When that is done, I load the form with the blank Report Viewer control on it.

Tell the ReportViewer1 where the local report is located, clear the local report DataSources, create a new DataSet, tell the new Dataset to read the Win32_Service is located and then add the DataSet.Tables(0) as a new LocalReport.DataSource using a new instance of Microsoft.Reporting.WinForms.ReportDataSource which requires the name of the internal name of the Dataset inside the rdlc file – which happens to be Dataset1 and the name of the Dataset followed by the table instance being used.

Here's the results:

AcceptPause	AcceptStop	Caption
FALSE	TRUE	AdobeUpdateService
FALSE	TRUE	Adobe Genuine Monitor Service
FALSE	TRUE	Adobe Genuine Software Integrity Service
FALSE	FALSE	AllJoyn Router Service
FALSE	FALSE	Application Layer Gateway Service
FALSE	TRUE	AMD External Events Utility
FALSE	TRUE	AMD Log Utility
FALSE	FALSE	Application Identity
FALSE	TRUE	Application Information
FALSE	FALSE	Application Management

WHY THE PROGRAM USES THE DATAGRIDVIEW

The DataGridView is used primarily to get an idea of exactly how wide each cell size is and then creating a decimal value of that data and dividing that by a number that most accurately matches the size in points for the rdlc field widths.

For me, this is one of the nice features of building rdlc reports on the fly because with the correct width, you don't have to go back and realign them.

Obviously, the population of the DataGridView can be done two ways. The first was used with populating it using the DataGridView DataSource with the DataSet.Tables(0) reference.

```
Me.Text = classname

Dim x As Integer = 0
Dim y As Integer = 0

Dim ds As New System.Data.DataSet
Dim dt As New System.Data.DataTable
ds.Tables.Add(dt)

Dim locator As New SWbemLocator
Dim svc As Object = locator.ConnectServer(".", ns)
Dim objs As Object = svc.InstancesOf(classname)
    For Each obj As SWbemObject In objs
        For Each prop As SWbemProperty In obj.Properties_
            DataGridView1.Columns.Add(prop.Name, prop.Name)
```

```
            Next
        . Exit For
    Next

    For Each obj As SWbemObject In objs
        DataGridView1.Rows.Add()
        For Each prop As SWbemProperty In obj.Properties_
            Dim tempstr As String = GetValue(prop.Name, obj)
            DataGridView1.Rows(y).Cells(x).Value = tempstr
            x = x + 1
        Next
        x = 0
        y = y + 1
    Next
```

The above code is how the DataGridView gets populated dynamically.

Now, let's add the logic to get the fields to look right when the report is being created:

```
    y = 0
    DataGridView1.AutoSizeColumnsMode = DataGridViewAutoSizeColumnMode.AllCells
    For y = 0 To DataGridView1.Columns.Count - 1
        Dim d As Double = (DataGridView1.Rows(0).Cells(y).Size.Width * 0.7675)
        Widthdic.Add(y, d.ToString())
    Next
```

Yes, I know it isn't 0.75 which would be the normal width converting pixels to points but there are also 2 points used to give space on the left and right of the data so, instead of making it so tight, I gave the math some room for those two spaces.

Anyway, here's the code that uses the code above, creates the xml and xsd files and calls for the creation of the report.

```
Private Sub Form2_Load(sender As Object, e As EventArgs) Handles MyBase.Load

    Me.Text = classname

    Dim x As Integer = 0
    Dim y As Integer = 0

    Dim ds As New System.Data.DataSet
    Dim dt As New System.Data.DataTable
```

```vb
        ds.Tables.Add(dt)


        rowdic = New System.Collections.Generic.Dictionary(Of Integer, System.Collections.Generic.Dictionary(Of Integer, String))
        Namesdic = New System.Collections.Generic.Dictionary(Of Integer, String)
        Widthdic = New System.Collections.Generic.Dictionary(Of Integer, String)


        Dim locator As New SWbemLocator
        Dim svc As Object = locator.ConnectServer(".", ns)
        Dim objs As Object = svc.InstancesOf(classname)

        If objs.Count = 1 Then

            Namesdic.Add(0, "Property Name")
            Namesdic.Add(1, "PropertyValue")

            ds.Tables(0).Columns.Add("PropertyName")
            DataGridView1.Columns.Add("PropertyName", "Property Name")

            ds.Tables(0).Columns.Add("PropertyValue")
            DataGridView1.Columns.Add("PropertyValue", "Property Value")


            For Each obj As SWbemObject In objs
                For Each prop As SWbemProperty In obj.Properties_
                    Dim Columndic As New System.Collections.Generic.Dictionary(Of Integer, String)
                    Dim dr As System.Data.DataRow = ds.Tables(0).NewRow()
                    DataGridView1.Rows.Add()
                    dr.Item(0) = prop.Name
                    DataGridView1.Rows(y).Cells(0).Value = prop.Name
                    Columndic.Add(0, prop.Name)
                    Dim tempstr As String = GetValue(prop.Name, obj)
                    dr.Item(1) = tempstr
                    DataGridView1.Rows(y).Cells(1).Value = tempstr
                    Columndic.Add(1, tempstr)
                    ds.Tables(0).Rows.Add(dr)
                    rowdic.Add(y, Columndic)
                    y = y + 1
                Next
            Next
```

```vb
ds.Tables(0).WriteXml(Application.StartupPath & "\" & classname & ".xml")
ds.Tables(0).WriteXmlSchema(Application.StartupPath & "\" & classname & ".xsd")
ds.Clear()


y = 0
DataGridView1.AutoSizeColumnsMode = DataGridViewAutoSizeColumnMode.AllCells
For y = 0 To DataGridView1.Columns.Count - 1
    Dim d As Double = (DataGridView1.Rows(0).Cells(y).Size.Width * 0.7675)
    Widthdic.Add(y, d.ToString())
Next

Else

    For Each obj As SWbemObject In objs
        For Each prop As SWbemProperty In obj.Properties_
            Try
                Namesdic.Add(x, prop.Name)
            Catch ex As Exception
                Namesdic.Add(x, "")
            End Try
            ds.Tables(0).Columns.Add(prop.Name)
            DataGridView1.Columns.Add(prop.Name, prop.Name)
            x = x + 1
        Next
        Exit For
    Next
    x = 0

    For Each obj As SWbemObject In objs

        Dim Columndic As New System.Collections.Generic.Dictionary(Of Integer, String)

        DataGridView1.Rows.Add()
        Dim dr As System.Data.DataRow = ds.Tables(0).NewRow()

        For Each prop As SWbemProperty In obj.Properties_

            Dim tempstr As String = GetValue(prop.Name, obj)

            dr.Item(x) = tempstr
            DataGridView1.Rows(y).Cells(x).Value = tempstr
            Columndic.Add(x, tempstr)
            x = x + 1
```

```vbnet
            Next
            ds.Tables(0).Rows.Add(dr)
            x = 0
            rowdic.Add(y, Columndic)
            y = y + 1
        Next

        ds.Tables(0).WriteXml(Application.StartupPath & "\" & classname & ".xml")
        ds.Tables(0).WriteXmlSchema(Application.StartupPath & "\" & classname & ".xsd")
        ds.Clear()

        y = 0
        DataGridView1.AutoSizeColumnsMode = DataGridViewAutoSizeColumnMode.AllCells
        For y = 0 To DataGridView1.Columns.Count - 1
            Dim d As Double = (DataGridView1.Rows(0).Cells(y).Size.Width * 0.7675)
            Widthdic.Add(y, d.ToString())
        Next


    End If

    Module1.Create_The_Report(classname)

End Sub
```

WHAT THE XML AND XSD LOOKS LIKE

While generating the XML and XSD for the WIN32_BIOS report, the XSD looks like this:

```
<?xml version="1.0" standalone="yes"?>
<xs:schema      id="NewDataSet"      xmlns=""      xmlns:xs="http://www.w3.org/2001/XMLSchema"
xmlns:msdata="urn:schemas-microsoft-com:xml-msdata">
    <xs:element      name="NewDataSet"      msdata:IsDataSet="true"      msdata:MainDataTable="Table1"
msdata:UseCurrentLocale="true">
      <xs:complexType>
       <xs:choice minOccurs="0" maxOccurs="unbounded">
        <xs:element name="Table1">
         <xs:complexType>
          <xs:sequence>
           <xs:element name="PropertyName" type="xs:string" minOccurs="0" />
           <xs:element name="PropertyValue" type="xs:string" minOccurs="0" />
          </xs:sequence>
         </xs:complexType>
        </xs:element>
       </xs:choice>
      </xs:complexType>
     </xs:element>
    </xs:schema>
```

The XML looks like this:

```xml
<?xml version="1.0" standalone="yes"?>
<NewDataSet>
 <Table1>
  <PropertyName>BiosCharacteristics</PropertyName>
  <PropertyValue>7, 10, 11, 12, 15, 16, 17, 19, 23, 24, 25, 26, 27, 28, 29, 32, 33, 40, 42, 43</PropertyValue>
 </Table1>
 <Table1>
  <PropertyName>BIOSVersion</PropertyName>
  <PropertyValue>ALASKA - 1072009, 0504, American Megatrends - 5000C</PropertyValue>
 </Table1>
 <Table1>
  <PropertyName>BuildNumber</PropertyName>
  <PropertyValue />
 </Table1>
 <Table1>
  <PropertyName>Caption</PropertyName>
  <PropertyValue>0504</PropertyValue>
 </Table1>
 <Table1>
  <PropertyName>CodeSet</PropertyName>
  <PropertyValue />
 </Table1>
 <Table1>
  <PropertyName>CurrentLanguage</PropertyName>
  <PropertyValue>en|US|iso8859-1</PropertyValue>
 </Table1>
 <Table1>
  <PropertyName>Description</PropertyName>
  <PropertyValue>0504</PropertyValue>
 </Table1>
 <Table1>
  <PropertyName>EmbeddedControllerMajorVersion</PropertyName>
  <PropertyValue>255</PropertyValue>
 </Table1>
 <Table1>
  <PropertyName>EmbeddedControllerMinorVersion</PropertyName>
  <PropertyValue>255</PropertyValue>
 </Table1>
 <Table1>
  <PropertyName>IdentificationCode</PropertyName>
  <PropertyValue />
```

```xml
    </Table1>
    <Table1>
     <PropertyName>InstallableLanguages</PropertyName>
     <PropertyValue>8</PropertyValue>
    </Table1>
    <Table1>
     <PropertyName>InstallDate</PropertyName>
     <PropertyValue />
    </Table1>
    <Table1>
     <PropertyName>LanguageEdition</PropertyName>
     <PropertyValue />
    </Table1>
    <Table1>
     <PropertyName>ListOfLanguages</PropertyName>
     <PropertyValue>en|US|iso8859-1, fr|FR|iso8859-1, zh|CN|unicode, , , ,</PropertyValue>
    </Table1>
    <Table1>
     <PropertyName>Manufacturer</PropertyName>
     <PropertyValue>American Megatrends Inc.</PropertyValue>
    </Table1>
    <Table1>
     <PropertyName>Name</PropertyName>
     <PropertyValue>0504</PropertyValue>
    </Table1>
    <Table1>
     <PropertyName>OtherTargetOS</PropertyName>
     <PropertyValue />
    </Table1>
    <Table1>
     <PropertyName>PrimaryBIOS</PropertyName>
     <PropertyValue>TRUE</PropertyValue>
    </Table1>
    <Table1>
     <PropertyName>ReleaseDate</PropertyName>
     <PropertyValue>24\02\2017 00:00:00</PropertyValue>
    </Table1>
    <Table1>
     <PropertyName>SerialNumber</PropertyName>
     <PropertyValue>System Serial Number</PropertyValue>
    </Table1>
    <Table1>
     <PropertyName>SMBIOSBIOSVersion</PropertyName>
     <PropertyValue>0504</PropertyValue>
```

```xml
    </Table1>
    <Table1>
      <PropertyName>SMBIOSMajorVersion</PropertyName>
      <PropertyValue>3</PropertyValue>
    </Table1>
    <Table1>
      <PropertyName>SMBIOSMinorVersion</PropertyName>
      <PropertyValue>0</PropertyValue>
    </Table1>
    <Table1>
      <PropertyName>SMBIOSPresent</PropertyName>
      <PropertyValue>TRUE</PropertyValue>
    </Table1>
    <Table1>
      <PropertyName>SoftwareElementID</PropertyName>
      <PropertyValue>0504</PropertyValue>
    </Table1>
    <Table1>
      <PropertyName>SoftwareElementState</PropertyName>
      <PropertyValue>3</PropertyValue>
    </Table1>
    <Table1>
      <PropertyName>Status</PropertyName>
      <PropertyValue>OK</PropertyValue>
    </Table1>
    <Table1>
      <PropertyName>SystemBiosMajorVersion</PropertyName>
      <PropertyValue>5</PropertyValue>
    </Table1>
    <Table1>
      <PropertyName>SystemBiosMinorVersion</PropertyName>
      <PropertyValue>12</PropertyValue>
    </Table1>
    <Table1>
      <PropertyName>TargetOperatingSystem</PropertyName>
      <PropertyValue>0</PropertyValue>
    </Table1>
    <Table1>
      <PropertyName>Version</PropertyName>
      <PropertyValue>ALASKA - 1072009</PropertyValue>
    </Table1>
  </NewDataSet>
```

CREATING THE RDLC REPORT DYNAMICALLY

This code is dynamically driven by the Names Dictionary and the Numbers Dictionary to fill in all the areas needed to marry up the field names with the xml data and adjust the widths to the correct sizes so that you don't have to ever have to modify the view.

Sound too good to be true?

Well, it is not too good to be true. It does exactly what was promised.

```
Public Sub Create_The_Report(ByVal ReportName As String)

        Dim fso As Object = CreateObject("Scripting.FileSystemObject")
        Dim txtstream As Object = fso.OpenTextFile(Application.StartupPath & "\" & ReportName & ".rdlc", 2,
True, -2)
        txtstream.WriteLine("<?xml version=""1.0"" encoding=""utf-8""?>")
        txtstream.WriteLine("<Report                                    xmlns                    =
""http://schemas.microsoft.com/sqlserver/reporting/2008/01/reportdefinition""          xmlns:rd           =
""http://schemas.microsoft.com/SQLServer/reporting/reportdesigner"" >")
        txtstream.WriteLine("   <Body>")
        txtstream.WriteLine("      <ReportItems>")
        txtstream.WriteLine("         <Tablix Name=""Tablix1"">")
        txtstream.WriteLine("            <TablixBody>")
        txtstream.WriteLine("               <TablixColumns>")
        For x As Integer = 0 To Namesdic.Count - 1
            txtstream.WriteLine("               <TablixColumn>")
            txtstream.WriteLine("                  <Width>" & Widthdic.Item(x).ToString() & "pt</Width>")
            txtstream.WriteLine("               </TablixColumn>")
        Next
        txtstream.WriteLine("            </TablixColumns>")
        txtstream.WriteLine("            <TablixRows>")
        txtstream.WriteLine("               <TablixRow>")
        txtstream.WriteLine("                  <Height>0.25in</Height>")
        txtstream.WriteLine("                  <TablixCells>")
```

```vbnet
For x As Integer = 0 To Namesdic.Count - 1
    txtstream.WriteLine("                        <TablixCell>")
    txtstream.WriteLine("                          <CellContents>")
    txtstream.WriteLine("                            <Textbox Name="""Textbox" & x & """">")
    txtstream.WriteLine("                              <CanGrow>true</CanGrow>")
    txtstream.WriteLine("                              <KeepTogether>true</KeepTogether>")
    txtstream.WriteLine("                              <Paragraphs>")
    txtstream.WriteLine("                                <Paragraph>")
    txtstream.WriteLine("                                  <TextRuns>")
    txtstream.WriteLine("                                    <TextRun>")
    txtstream.WriteLine("                                      <Value>" & Namesdic.Item(x).ToString()
& "</Value>")
    txtstream.WriteLine("                                      <Style>")
    txtstream.WriteLine("                                        <FontSize>8pt</FontSize>")
    txtstream.WriteLine("                                        <FontWeight>Bold</FontWeight>")
    txtstream.WriteLine("                                        <Color>White</Color>")
    txtstream.WriteLine("                                      </Style>")
    txtstream.WriteLine("                                    </TextRun>")
    txtstream.WriteLine("                                  </TextRuns>")
    txtstream.WriteLine("                                  <Style>")
    txtstream.WriteLine("                                    <TextAlign>Left</TextAlign>")
    txtstream.WriteLine("                                  </Style>")
    txtstream.WriteLine("                                </Paragraph>")
    txtstream.WriteLine("                              </Paragraphs>")
    txtstream.WriteLine("                            <rd:DefaultName>Textbox" & x & "</rd:DefaultName>")
    txtstream.WriteLine("                              <Style>")
    txtstream.WriteLine("                                <Border>")
    txtstream.WriteLine("                                  <Style>None</Style>")
    txtstream.WriteLine("                                </Border>")
    txtstream.WriteLine("                                <BottomBorder>")
    txtstream.WriteLine("                                  <Color>LightGrey</Color>")
    txtstream.WriteLine("                                  <Style>Solid</Style>")
    txtstream.WriteLine("                                  <Width>1pt</Width>")
    txtstream.WriteLine("                                </BottomBorder>")
    txtstream.WriteLine("
<BackgroundColor>MidnightBlue</BackgroundColor>")
    txtstream.WriteLine("                                <PaddingLeft>2pt</PaddingLeft>")
    txtstream.WriteLine("                                <PaddingRight>2pt</PaddingRight>")
    txtstream.WriteLine("                                <PaddingTop>2pt</PaddingTop>")
    txtstream.WriteLine("                                <PaddingBottom>2pt</PaddingBottom>")
    txtstream.WriteLine("                              </Style>")
    txtstream.WriteLine("                            </Textbox>")
    txtstream.WriteLine("                            <rd:Selected>true</rd:Selected>")
    txtstream.WriteLine("                          </CellContents>")
```

```vb
            txtstream.WriteLine("                                    </TablixCell>")
        Next


            txtstream.WriteLine("                                </TablixCells>")
            txtstream.WriteLine("                            </TablixRow>")
            txtstream.WriteLine("                            <TablixRow>")
            txtstream.WriteLine("                                <Height>0.25in</Height>")
            txtstream.WriteLine("                                <TablixCells>")
        For x As Integer = 0 To Namesdic.Count - 1
            txtstream.WriteLine("                                    <TablixCell>")
            txtstream.WriteLine("                                        <CellContents>")
            txtstream.WriteLine("                                            <Textbox Name=""" & Namesdic.Item(x).ToString()
& """>")
            txtstream.WriteLine("                                                <CanGrow>true</CanGrow>")
            txtstream.WriteLine("                                                <KeepTogether>true</KeepTogether>")
            txtstream.WriteLine("                                                <Paragraphs>")
            txtstream.WriteLine("                                                  <Paragraph>")
            txtstream.WriteLine("                                                    <TextRuns>")
            txtstream.WriteLine("                                                      <TextRun>")
            txtstream.WriteLine("                                                        <Value>=Fields!" & Namesdic.Item(x).ToString()
& ".Value</Value>")
            txtstream.WriteLine("                                                        <Style>")
            txtstream.WriteLine("                                                          <FontSize>8pt</FontSize>")
            txtstream.WriteLine("                                                          <FontWeight>Normal</FontWeight>")
            txtstream.WriteLine("                                                          <Color>#333333</Color>")
            txtstream.WriteLine("                                                        </Style>")
            txtstream.WriteLine("                                                      </TextRun>")
            txtstream.WriteLine("                                                    </TextRuns>")
            txtstream.WriteLine("                                                    <Style/>")
            txtstream.WriteLine("                                                  </Paragraph>")
            txtstream.WriteLine("                                                </Paragraphs>")
            txtstream.WriteLine("                                                <rd:DefaultName>" & Namesdic.Item(x).ToString()
& "</rd:DefaultName>")
            txtstream.WriteLine("                                                <Style>")
            txtstream.WriteLine("                                                  <Border>")
            txtstream.WriteLine("                                                    <Style>None</Style>")
            txtstream.WriteLine("                                                  </Border>")
            txtstream.WriteLine("                                                  <BackgroundColor>White</BackgroundColor>")
            txtstream.WriteLine("                                                  <PaddingLeft>2pt</PaddingLeft>")
            txtstream.WriteLine("                                                  <PaddingRight>2pt</PaddingRight>")
            txtstream.WriteLine("                                                  <PaddingTop>2pt</PaddingTop>")
            txtstream.WriteLine("                                                  <PaddingBottom>2pt</PaddingBottom>")
            txtstream.WriteLine("                                                </Style>")
```

```vb
            txtstream.WriteLine("                           </Textbox>")
            txtstream.WriteLine("                         </CellContents>")
            txtstream.WriteLine("                       </TablixCell>")
Next
        txtstream.WriteLine("                   </TablixCells>")
        txtstream.WriteLine("                 </TablixRow>")
        txtstream.WriteLine("               </TablixRows>")
        txtstream.WriteLine("             </TablixBody>")
        txtstream.WriteLine("             <TablixColumnHierarchy>")
        txtstream.WriteLine("               <TablixMembers>")
For x As Integer = 0 To Namesdic.Count - 1
        txtstream.WriteLine("                 <TablixMember/>")
Next
        txtstream.WriteLine("               </TablixMembers>")
        txtstream.WriteLine("             </TablixColumnHierarchy>")
        txtstream.WriteLine("             <TablixRowHierarchy>")
        txtstream.WriteLine("               <TablixMembers>")
        txtstream.WriteLine("                 <TablixMember>")
        txtstream.WriteLine("                   <KeepWithGroup>After</KeepWithGroup>")
        txtstream.WriteLine("                 </TablixMember>")
        txtstream.WriteLine("                 <TablixMember>")
        txtstream.WriteLine("                   <Group Name=""Details""/>")
        txtstream.WriteLine("                 </TablixMember>")
        txtstream.WriteLine("               </TablixMembers>")
        txtstream.WriteLine("             </TablixRowHierarchy>")
        txtstream.WriteLine("             <DataSetName>DataSet1</DataSetName>")
        txtstream.WriteLine("             <Height>0.5in</Height>")
        txtstream.WriteLine("             <Width>141.11459in</Width>")
        txtstream.WriteLine("             <Style>")
        txtstream.WriteLine("               <Border>")
        txtstream.WriteLine("                 <Style>None</Style>")
        txtstream.WriteLine("               </Border>")
        txtstream.WriteLine("             </Style>")
        txtstream.WriteLine("           </Tablix>")
        txtstream.WriteLine("         </ReportItems>")
        txtstream.WriteLine("         <Height>2in</Height>")
        txtstream.WriteLine("         <Style/>")
        txtstream.WriteLine("       </Body>")
        txtstream.WriteLine("     <Width>141.11459in</Width>")
        txtstream.WriteLine("     <Page>")
        txtstream.WriteLine("       <LeftMargin>1in</LeftMargin>")
        txtstream.WriteLine("       <RightMargin>1in</RightMargin>")
        txtstream.WriteLine("       <TopMargin>1in</TopMargin>")
        txtstream.WriteLine("       <BottomMargin>1in</BottomMargin>")
```

```vbnet
        txtstream.WriteLine("    <Style />")
        txtstream.WriteLine("  </Page>")
        txtstream.WriteLine("  <AutoRefresh>0</AutoRefresh>")
        txtstream.WriteLine("  <DataSources>")
        txtstream.WriteLine("    <DataSource Name = """"NewDataSet"""" >")
        txtstream.WriteLine("      <ConnectionProperties>")
        txtstream.WriteLine("        <DataProvider>System.Data.DataSet</DataProvider>")
        txtstream.WriteLine("        <ConnectString>/* Local Connection */</ConnectString>")
        txtstream.WriteLine("      </ConnectionProperties>")
        txtstream.WriteLine("                                  <rd:DataSourceID>41290037-fb2a-40cc-8d26-
595fc960f58f</rd:DataSourceID>")
        txtstream.WriteLine("    </DataSource>")
        txtstream.WriteLine("  </DataSources>")
        txtstream.WriteLine("  <DataSets>")
        txtstream.WriteLine("    <DataSet Name = """"DataSet1"""" >")
        txtstream.WriteLine("      <Query>")
        txtstream.WriteLine("        <DataSourceName>NewDataSet</DataSourceName>")
        txtstream.WriteLine("        <CommandText>/* Local Query */</CommandText>")
        txtstream.WriteLine("      </Query>")
        txtstream.WriteLine("      <Fields>")

        For x As Integer = 0 To Namesdic.Count - 1
            txtstream.WriteLine("        <Field Name = """ & Namesdic.Item(x).ToString() & """ >")
            txtstream.WriteLine("          <DataField>" & Namesdic.Item(x).ToString() & "</DataField>")
            txtstream.WriteLine("          <rd:TypeName>System.String</rd:TypeName>")
            txtstream.WriteLine("        </Field>")
        Next

        txtstream.WriteLine("      </Fields>")
        txtstream.WriteLine("      <rd:DataSetInfo>")
        txtstream.WriteLine("        <rd:DataSetName>NewDataSet</rd:DataSetName>")
        txtstream.WriteLine("        <rd:SchemaPath>" & Application.StartupPath & "\" & classname &
".xsd</rd:SchemaPath>")
        txtstream.WriteLine("        <rd:TableName>Table1</rd:TableName>")
        txtstream.WriteLine("      </rd:DataSetInfo>")
        txtstream.WriteLine("    </DataSet>")
        txtstream.WriteLine("  </DataSets>")
        txtstream.WriteLine("  <rd:ReportUnitType> Inch</rd:ReportUnitType>")
        txtstream.WriteLine("  <rd:ReportID>24f3cae4-fa56-46ac-a966-3f8e0c79ee36</rd:ReportID>")
        txtstream.WriteLine("</Report>")
        txtstream.Close()

    End Sub
```

End Module

Notice that the code doesn't care if we are wanting a vertical or horizontal rendering. When all this code is running, you end up with reports that look like this:

PropertyName	PropertyValue
BiosCharacteristics	7, 10, 11, 12, 15, 16, 17, 19, 23, 24, 25, 26, 27, 28, 29, 32, 33, 40, 42, 43
BIOSVersion	ALASKA - 1072009, 0504, American Megatrends - 5000C
BuildNumber	
Caption	0504
CodeSet	
CurrentLanguage	en|US|iso8859-1
Description	0504
EmbeddedControllerMajorVersion	255
EmbeddedControllerMinorVersion	255
IdentificationCode	
InstallableLanguages	8
InstallDate	
LanguageEdition	
ListOfLanguages	en|US|iso8859-1, fr|FR|iso8859-1, zh|CN|unicode, , , , ,
Manufacturer	American Megatrends Inc.
Name	0504
OtherTargetOS	
PrimaryBIOS	TRUE
ReleaseDate	24\02\2017 00:00:00
SerialNumber	System Serial Number
SMBIOSBIOSVersion	0504
SMBIOSMajorVersion	3
SMBIOSMinorVersion	0
SMBIOSPresent	TRUE
SoftwareElementID	0504
SoftwareElementState	3
Status	OK
SystemBiosMajorVersion	5
SystemBiosMinorVersion	12
TargetOperatingSystem	0
Version	ALASKA - 1072009

GLEANING INFORMATION FROM EVENT LOGS USING WMI

WMI has a couple of EventLog classes that will help us create reports from the information contained within the event logs.

Win32_NTEventLogFile, Win32_NTLogEventLog and Win32_NTLogEvent.

The Win32_NTEvetLogFile exposes the following properties:

AccessMask
Archive
Caption
Compressed
CompressionMethod
CreationClassName
CreationDate
CSCreationClassName
CSName
Description
Drive
EightDotThreeFileName
Encrypted
EncryptionMethod
Extension
FileName

FileSize

FileType

FSCreationClassName

FSName

Hidden

InstallDate

InUseCount

LastAccessed

LastModified

LogfileName

Manufacturer

MaxFileSize

Name

NumberOfRecords

OverwriteOutDated

OverWritePolicy

Path

Readable

Sources

Status

System

Version

Writeable

The Win32_NTLogEventLog exposes the following properties:

Log

Record

The Win32_NTLogEvent exposes the following properties:

Category

CategoryString

ComputerName

Data

EventCode

EventIdentifier

EventType

InsertionStrings

Logfile

Message

RecordNumber

SourceName

TimeGenerated

TimeWritten

Type

User

Okay, so the first thing we want to do is create a report from the Win32_NTEvetLogFile:

```
Imports WbemScripting

Public Class Form1
    Private Function GetValue(ByVal n As String, ByVal obj As Object)

        Dim tempstr As String = ""
        Dim pName As String = vbTab & n & " = "
        tempstr = obj.GetObjectText_!
        Dim pos As Integer = InStr(tempstr, pName)

        If pos > 0 Then

            pos = pos + Len(vbTab & n & " = ")
            tempstr = Mid(tempstr, pos, Len(tempstr))
            pos = InStr(tempstr, ";")
            tempstr = Mid(tempstr, 1, pos - 1)
            tempstr = Replace(tempstr, Chr(34), "")
            tempstr = Replace(tempstr, "{", "")
```

```vbnet
        tempstr = Replace(tempstr, "}", "")
        tempstr = Trim(tempstr)


        If (obj.Properties_.Item(n).CIMType = WbemCimtypeEnum.wbemCimtypeDatetime AndAlso
Len(tempstr) > 14) Then
            tempstr = Mid(tempstr, 7, 2) + "\" + Mid(tempstr, 5, 2) + "\" + Mid(tempstr, 1, 4) + " " +
Mid(tempstr, 9, 2) + ":" + Mid(tempstr, 11, 2) + ":" + Mid(tempstr, 13, 2)
        End If



    Else

        tempstr = ""

    End If



    Return tempstr



End Function

Private Sub Form1_Load(sender As Object, e As EventArgs) Handles MyBase.Load

    'ToolStripComboBox1.Text = "*Select A Log File*"
    'ToolStripComboBox1.Items.Add("*Select A Log File*")
    Dim loc As Object = CreateObject("WbemScripting.SWbemLocator")
    Dim svc As Object = loc.ConnectServer(".", "root\CIMV2")
    Dim objs As Object = svc.ExecQuery("Select * from Win32_NTEventLogFile")

    classname = "Win32_NTEventLogFile"


    Me.Text = classname

    Dim x As Integer = 0
    Dim y As Integer = 0

    Dim ds As New System.Data.DataSet
    Dim dt As New System.Data.DataTable
    ds.Tables.Add(dt)
```

```vbnet
rowdic          =          New          System.Collections.Generic.Dictionary(Of          Integer,
System.Collections.Generic.Dictionary(Of Integer, String))
    Namesdic = New System.Collections.Generic.Dictionary(Of Integer, String)
    Widthdic = New System.Collections.Generic.Dictionary(Of Integer, String)


    For Each obj As SWbemObject In objs
      For Each prop As SWbemProperty In obj.Properties_
        If IsDBNull(prop.Value) = False Then
          Try
            Namesdic.Add(x, prop.Name)
          Catch ex As Exception
            Namesdic.Add(x, "")
          End Try
          ds.Tables(0).Columns.Add(prop.Name)
          DataGridView1.Columns.Add(prop.Name, prop.Name)
          x = x + 1
        End If
      Next
      x = 0
      Exit For
    Next


    For Each obj As SWbemObject In objs
      Dim Columndic As New System.Collections.Generic.Dictionary(Of Integer, String)
      DataGridView1.Rows.Add()
      Dim dr As System.Data.DataRow = ds.Tables(0).NewRow()
      For Each prop As SWbemProperty In obj.Properties_
        If IsDBNull(prop.Value) = False Then
          Dim tempstr As String = GetValue(prop.Name, obj)
          dr.Item(x) = tempstr
          DataGridView1.Rows(y).Cells(x).Value = tempstr
          Columndic.Add(x, tempstr)
          x = x + 1
        End If
      Next
      ds.Tables(0).Rows.Add(dr)
      x = 0
      rowdic.Add(y, Columndic)
      y = y + 1
    Next


    ds.Tables(0).WriteXml(Application.StartupPath & "\" & classname & ".xml")
```

```
ds.Tables(0).WriteXmlSchema(Application.StartupPath & "\" & classname & ".xsd")
ds.Clear()
y = 0
DataGridView1.AutoSizeColumnsMode = DataGridViewAutoSizeColumnMode.AllCells
For y = 0 To DataGridView1.Columns.Count - 1
    Dim d As Double = (DataGridView1.Rows(0).Cells(y).Size.Width * 0.785)
    Widthdic.Add(y, d.ToString())
Next

Module1.Create_The_Report(classname)

Dim ds1 As New System.Data.DataSet
Dim myform As New Form3
myform.Text = "Win32_NTEventLogFile"
myform.ReportViewer1.LocalReport.ReportPath = Application.StartupPath & "\" & classname &
".rdlc"
myform.ReportViewer1.LocalReport.DataSources.Clear()
ds1.ReadXml(Application.StartupPath & "\" & classname & ".xml")
myform.ReportViewer1.LocalReport.DataSources.Add(New
Microsoft.Reporting.WinForms.ReportDataSource("DataSet1", ds1.Tables(0)))
myform.ReportViewer1.RefreshReport()
myform.Show()

    End Sub
End Class
```

Since the creation of the report doesn't change, I see no reason why it needs to be added here as it has already been added to this book and I want to save enough space in this book to cover creating reports using the WMI Registry Provider.

The DataGridView output looks like this:

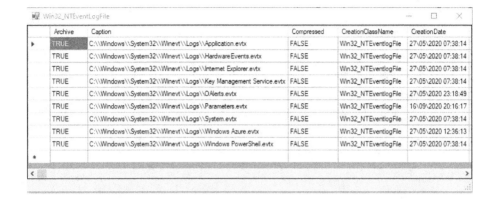

And the Report:

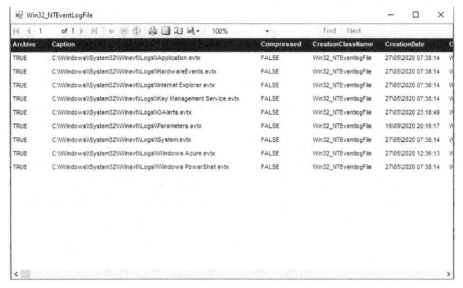

WORKING WITH THE Win32_NTLogEvent

Now, we have our work cut out for us.

Why?

Because we need to be able to create a query string that pulls back exactly what we want to see verses what is being shown by default.

Category
CategoryString
ComputerName
Data
EventCode
EventIdentifier
EventType
InsertionStrings
Logfile
Message
RecordNumber
SourceName
TimeGenerated
TimeWritten
Type
User

Obviously, the logfile has to be part of the query. Beyond that, the type or severity of the event limits what is being returned as well as the SourceName – also known as the publisher – is important, too.

But the two that begs to be included is the TimeGenerated or the TimeWritten.

Take a look at the date in the bottom right hand corner of the image below where the task bar is telling me what time it was on my machine and the events were generated as recorded in the TimeGenerated and the TimeWritten.

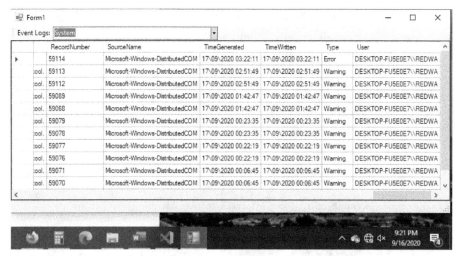

Don't you just love hackers?

Anyway, so I created a form that looks like this:

The biggest thing here is to remember to put the date in the right format: yyyymmdd and Start and end it with a double quote. Looks like this "20200917".

Also, I found the = to be not enough, so I used the >= instead and that worked.

Once the DataGridView is populated, the program creates the report. You can move that code to somewhere else if you like. Everything needed to create the report view has already been created.

So you can put another button on the form and when you click the button, after you have moved the code under it, it will do the same thing as it is currently doing inside the create the query routine is currently doing.

Form3 which is used the show the report, is the parent for the ReportViewer control and has no code under it

Here's the complete code for form 2:

```
Imports WbemScripting
Public Class Form2
    Private Function GetValue(ByVal n As String, ByVal obj As Object)

        Dim tempstr As String = ""
        Dim pName As String = vbTab & n & " = "
        tempstr = obj.GetObjectText_!
        Dim pos As Integer = InStr(tempstr, pName)

        If pos > 0 Then

            pos = pos + Len(vbTab & n & " = ")
            tempstr = Mid(tempstr, pos, Len(tempstr))
            pos = InStr(tempstr, ";")
            tempstr = Mid(tempstr, 1, pos - 1)
            tempstr = Replace(tempstr, Chr(34), "")
            tempstr = Replace(tempstr, "{", "")
            tempstr = Replace(tempstr, "}", "")
            tempstr = Trim(tempstr)

            If (obj.Properties_.Item(n).CIMType = WbemCimtypeEnum.wbemCimtypeDatetime AndAlso Len(tempstr) > 14) Then
                tempstr = Mid(tempstr, 7, 2) + "\" + Mid(tempstr, 5, 2) + "\" + Mid(tempstr, 1, 4) + " " + Mid(tempstr, 9, 2) + ":" + Mid(tempstr, 11, 2) + ":" + Mid(tempstr, 13, 2)
            End If

        Else

            tempstr = ""

        End If


        Return tempstr
```

```vb
        End Function
    Private Sub Form2_Load(sender As Object, e As EventArgs) Handles MyBase.Load
        ToolStripComboBox1.Text = "*Select A Log File*"
        ToolStripComboBox1.Items.Add("*Select A Log File*")
        Dim loc As Object = CreateObject("WbemScripting.SWbemLocator")
        Dim svc As Object = loc.ConnectServer(".", "root\CIMV2")
        Dim objs As Object = svc.ExecQuery("Select LogfileName from Win32_NTEventLogFile where
NumberOfRecords > 0")
        For Each obj In objs
            ToolStripComboBox1.Items.Add(obj.LogFileName)
        Next
    End Sub

    Private Sub ToolStripComboBox1_SelectedIndexChanged(sender As Object, e As EventArgs) Handles
ToolStripComboBox1.SelectedIndexChanged
        If ToolStripComboBox1.Text = "*Select A Log File*" Then Exit Sub

        ToolStripComboBox3.Items.Clear()
        ToolStripComboBox3.Text = "*Select A Source*"
        ToolStripComboBox3.Items.Add("*Select A Source*")
        Dim loc As Object = CreateObject("WbemScripting.SWbemLocator")
        Dim svc As Object = loc.ConnectServer(".", "root\CIMV2")
        Dim objs As Object = svc.ExecQuery("Select Sources from Win32_NTEventLogFile where LogFileName = '" &
ToolStripComboBox1.Text & "'")
        For Each obj In objs
            Dim mysources() As Object = obj.Sources
            For x As Integer = 0 To UBound(mysources) - 1
                ToolStripComboBox3.Items.Add(mysources(x).ToString())
            Next
        Next

    End Sub

    Private Sub ToolStripComboBox3_SelectedIndexChanged(sender As Object, e As EventArgs) Handles
ToolStripComboBox3.SelectedIndexChanged


    End Sub

    Private Sub ToolStripButton1_Click(sender As Object, e As EventArgs) Handles ToolStripButton1.Click
```

```vbnet
Dim tempstr As String = "Select * From Win32_NTLogEvent where LogFile = '" & ToolStripComboBox1.Text
& "'"
    If ToolStripComboBox3.Text <> "*Select A Source*" Then
        tempstr = tempstr & " and SourceName = '" & ToolStripComboBox3.Text & "'"
    End If
    If ToolStripComboBox2.Text <> "*Select A Type*" Then

        Select Case ToolStripComboBox2.Text
            Case "1 - Error"
                tempstr = tempstr & " and EventType=1"
            Case "2 - Warning"
                tempstr = tempstr & " and EventType=2"
            Case "3 - Information"
                tempstr = tempstr & " and EventType=3"
            Case "4 - Security Audit Success"
                tempstr = tempstr & " and EventType=4"
            Case "5 - Security Audit Fail"
                tempstr = tempstr & " and EventType=16"

        End Select

    End If

    If ToolStripComboBox4.Text <> "*Select An Option*" AndAlso ToolStripTextBox1.Text <> "" Then
        tempstr = tempstr & " and TimeGenerated " & ToolStripComboBox4.Text & " " & ToolStripTextBox1.Text &
" "
    End If

    If ToolStripComboBox5.Text <> "*Select An Option*" AndAlso ToolStripTextBox2.Text <> "" Then
        tempstr = tempstr & " and TimeWritten " & ToolStripComboBox5.Text & " " & ToolStripTextBox2.Text & "
"
    End If


    Dim ds As New System.Data.DataSet
    Dim dt As New System.Data.DataTable
    ds.Tables.Add(dt)


    Namesdic = New System.Collections.Generic.Dictionary(Of Integer, String)
    Widthdic = New System.Collections.Generic.Dictionary(Of Integer, String)


    Dim x As Integer = 0
```

```vb
Dim loc As Object = CreateObject("WbemScripting.SWbemLocator")
Dim svc As Object = loc.ConnectServer(".", "root\CIMV2")
Dim objs As Object = svc.ExecQuery(tempstr)
DataGridView1.Rows.Clear()
DataGridView1.Columns.Clear()
For Each obj In objs
    For Each prop In obj.Properties_
        Namesdic.Add(x, prop.Name)
        ds.Tables(0).Columns.Add(prop.Name)
        DataGridView1.Columns.Add(prop.Name, prop.Name)
        x = x + 1
    Next
    Exit For
Next

x = 0

Dim y As Integer = 0

For Each obj In objs
    DataGridView1.Rows.Add()
    Dim dr As System.Data.DataRow = ds.Tables(0).NewRow
    For Each prop In obj.Properties_
        Dim value As String = GetValue(prop.Name, obj)
        dr.Item(prop.Name) = value
        DataGridView1.Rows(y).Cells(x).Value = value
        Application.DoEvents()
        x = x + 1
    Next
    ds.Tables(0).Rows.Add(dr)
    x = 0
    y = y + 1
Next

ds.Tables(0).WriteXml(Application.StartupPath & "\Win32_NTLogEvent.xml")
ds.Tables(0).WriteXmlSchema(Application.StartupPath & "\Win32_NTLogEvent.xsd")
ds.Clear()

classname = "Win32_NTLogEvent"

y = 0
DataGridView1.AutoSizeColumnsMode = DataGridViewAutoSizeColumnMode.AllCells
For y = 0 To DataGridView1.Columns.Count - 1
```

```
    Dim d As Double = (DataGridView1.Rows(0).Cells(y).Size.Width * 0.785)
    Widthdic.Add(y, d.ToString())
Next

Module1.Create_The_Report(classname)
```

This is the code that can be moved to anywhere as long as the above code has already been run. You may want to do this so that you can work with the code above. And then run the report when you need to.

```
    Dim ds1 As New System.Data.DataSet
    Dim myform As New Form3
    myform.Text = "Win32_NTLogEvent"
    myform.ReportViewer1.LocalReport.ReportPath = Application.StartupPath & "\Win32_NTLogEvent.rdlc"
    myform.ReportViewer1.LocalReport.DataSources.Clear()
    ds1.ReadXml(Application.StartupPath & "\Win32_NTLogEvent.xml")
    myform.ReportViewer1.LocalReport.DataSources.Add(New
Microsoft.Reporting.WinForms.ReportDataSource("DataSet1", ds1.Tables(0)))
    myform.ReportViewer1.RefreshReport()
    myform.Show()
```

The above last line is the end of the code that can be moved.

```
    End Sub

End Class
```

CREATING REPORTS USING THE WMI REGISTRY PROVIDER

Imagine, for a moment, your boss comes walking over to you and says to you that he needs a report made form the information in the registry from a key and all its values.

You would probably look at him like he was stark raving mad. After all, as you've been told, one key deleted could mean you have to rebuild your machine or have someone else rebuild it.

Well, relax. Just about the only thing you have to worry about with the code about to be revealed to you that it can do is not work as expected and you would have to lean how to tweak it.

```
Imports WbemScripting
Public Class Form1
    Dim oReg As SWbemObject
    Const HKEY_CLASSES_ROOT = &H80000000
    Const HKEY_CURRENT_CONFIG = &H80000005
    Const HKEY_CURRENT_USER = &H80000001
    Const HKEY_LOCAL_MACHINE = &H80000002
    Const HKEY_USERS = &H80000003

    Private Sub Form1_Load(sender As Object, e As EventArgs) Handles MyBase.Load

        oReg = GetObject("winmgmts:\\.\root\Default:StdRegProv")
```

```vbnet
        End Sub

    Private Sub ToolStripComboBox1_SelectedIndexChanged(sender As Object, e As EventArgs) Handles
ToolStripComboBox1.SelectedIndexChanged

        If ToolStripComboBox1.Text = "*Select A Hive*" Then Exit Sub

        Dim myarray() As Object = Nothing

        Select Case ToolStripComboBox1.Text

            Case "HKEY_CLASSES_ROOT"

                Dim inparams As SWbemObject = oReg.Methods_.Item("EnumKey").InParameters
                Dim outparams As SWbemObject = oReg.Methods_.Item("EnumKey").OutParameters
                inparams.hDefKey = HKEY_CLASSES_ROOT
                inparams.sSubkeyName = ""
                outparams = oReg.ExecMethod_("EnumKey", inparams)
                myarray = outparams.sNames

            Case "HKEY_CURRENT_CONFIG"

                Dim inparams As SWbemObject = oReg.Methods_.Item("EnumKey").InParameters
                Dim outparams As SWbemObject = oReg.Methods_.Item("EnumKey").OutParameters
                inparams.hDefKey = HKEY_CURRENT_CONFIG
                inparams.sSubkeyName = ""
                outparams = oReg.ExecMethod_("EnumKey", inparams)
                myarray = outparams.sNames

            Case "HKEY_CURRENT_USER"

                Dim inparams As SWbemObject = oReg.Methods_.Item("EnumKey").InParameters
                Dim outparams As SWbemObject = oReg.Methods_.Item("EnumKey").OutParameters
                inparams.hDefKey = HKEY_CURRENT_USER
                inparams.sSubkeyName = ""
                outparams = oReg.ExecMethod_("EnumKey", inparams)
                myarray = outparams.sNames

            Case "HKEY_LOCAL_MACHINE"

                Dim inparams As SWbemObject = oReg.Methods_.Item("EnumKey").InParameters
                Dim outparams As SWbemObject = oReg.Methods_.Item("EnumKey").OutParameters
```

```vbnet
                    inparams.hDefKey = HKEY_LOCAL__MACHINE
                    inparams.sSubkeyName = ""
                    outparams = oReg.ExecMethod_("EnumKey", inparams)
                    myarray = outparams.sNames

                Case "HKEY_USERS"

                    Dim inparams As SWbemObject = oReg.Methods_.Item("EnumKey").InParameters
                    Dim outparams As SWbemObject = oReg.Methods_.Item("EnumKey").OutParameters
                    inparams.hDefKey = HKEY_USERS
                    inparams.sSubkeyName = ""
                    outparams = oReg.ExecMethod_("EnumKey", inparams)
                    myarray = outparams.sNames

            End Select

            TreeView1.Nodes.Clear()

            For x As Integer = 0 To UBound(myarray)
                TreeView1.Nodes.Add(myarray(x).ToString)
            Next

    End Sub

    Private Sub TreeView1_AfterSelect(sender As Object, e As TreeViewEventArgs) Handles
TreeView1.AfterSelect

        If TreeView1.SelectedNode.Nodes.Count = 0 Then

            Dim myarray() As Object

            Try
                oReg = GetObject("winmgmts:\\.\root\Default:StdRegProv")

                Select Case ToolStripComboBox1.Text

                    Case "HKEY_CLASSES_ROOT"

                        Dim inparams As SWbemObject = oReg.Methods_.Item("EnumKey").InParameters
                        Dim outparams As SWbemObject = oReg.Methods_.Item("EnumKey").OutParameters
                        inparams.hDefKey = HKEY_CLASSES_ROOT
                        inparams.sSubkeyName = TreeView1.SelectedNode.FullPath
                        outparams = oReg.ExecMethod_("EnumKey", inparams)
                        myarray = outparams.sNames
```

```vbnet
        Case "HKEY_CURRENT_CONFIG"

            Dim inparams As SWbemObject = oReg.Methods_.Item("EnumKey").InParameters
            Dim outparams As SWbemObject = oReg.Methods_.Item("EnumKey").OutParameters
            inparams.hDefKey = HKEY_CURRENT_CONFIG
            inparams.sSubkeyName = TreeView1.SelectedNode.FullPath
            outparams = oReg.ExecMethod_("EnumKey", inparams)
            myarray = outparams.sNames

        Case "HKEY_CURRENT_USER"

            Dim inparams As SWbemObject = oReg.Methods_.Item("EnumKey").InParameters
            Dim outparams As SWbemObject = oReg.Methods_.Item("EnumKey").OutParameters
            inparams.hDefKey = HKEY_CURRENT_USER
            inparams.sSubkeyName = TreeView1.SelectedNode.FullPath
            outparams = oReg.ExecMethod_("EnumKey", inparams)
            myarray = outparams.sNames

        Case "HKEY_LOCAL_MACHINE"

            Dim inparams As SWbemObject = oReg.Methods_.Item("EnumKey").InParameters
            Dim outparams As SWbemObject = oReg.Methods_.Item("EnumKey").OutParameters
            inparams.hDefKey = HKEY_LOCAL_MACHINE
            inparams.sSubkeyName = TreeView1.SelectedNode.FullPath
            outparams = oReg.ExecMethod_("EnumKey", inparams)
            myarray = outparams.sNames

        Case "HKEY_USERS"

            Dim inparams As SWbemObject = oReg.Methods_.Item("EnumKey").InParameters
            Dim outparams As SWbemObject = oReg.Methods_.Item("EnumKey").OutParameters
            inparams.hDefKey = HKEY_USERS
            inparams.sSubkeyName = TreeView1.SelectedNode.FullPath
            outparams = oReg.ExecMethod_("EnumKey", inparams)
            myarray = outparams.sNames

    End Select

    For x As Integer = 0 To UBound(myarray)
        TreeView1.SelectedNode.Nodes.Add(myarray(x).ToString)
    Next
```

```vbnet
        Catch

            Err.Clear()

        End Try

    End If

    GetValues()

End Sub

Public Sub GetValues()


    Dim myTypes
    Dim myarray
    Dim y As Integer = 0

    DataGridView1.Rows.Clear()

    oReg = GetObject("winmgmts:\\.\root\Default:StdRegProv")

    Select Case ToolStripComboBox1.Text

        Case "HKEY_CLASSES_ROOT"

            Dim inparams As SWbemObject = oReg.Methods_.Item("EnumValues").InParameters
            Dim outparams As SWbemObject = oReg.Methods_.Item("EnumValues").OutParameters
            inparams.hDefKey = HKEY_CLASSES_ROOT
            inparams.sSubkeyName = TreeView1.SelectedNode.FullPath
            outparams = oReg.ExecMethod_("EnumValues", inparams,)
            myarray = outparams.Properties_.Item("sNames").Value
            myTypes = outparams.Properties_.Item("Types").Value


            If IsDBNull(myTypes) = True Then

                Try

                    Dim strValue As Object = ""
                    oReg.GetStringValue(HKEY_CLASSES_ROOT,    TreeView1.SelectedNode.FullPath,    "",
strValue)
                    DataGridView1.Rows.Add()
```

```vbnet
                DataGridView1.Rows(y).Cells(0).Value = "(Default)"
                DataGridView1.Rows(y).Cells(1).Value = "REG_SZ"
                DataGridView1.Rows(y).Cells(2).Value = strValue
                y = y + 1
            Catch


            End Try

            Exit Sub

        End If

        For x As Integer = 0 To UBound(myTypes)

            Select Case myTypes(x)

                Case 1

                    Dim strValue As Object = ""
                    Dim Name As String = myarray(x)
                    oReg.GetStringValue(HKEY_CLASSES_ROOT,        TreeView1.SelectedNode.FullPath,
Name, strValue)
                    DataGridView1.Rows.Add()
                    DataGridView1.Rows(y).Cells(0).Value = Name
                    DataGridView1.Rows(y).Cells(1).Value = "REG_SZ"
                    DataGridView1.Rows(y).Cells(2).Value = strValue.ToString()
                    y = y + 1

                Case 2

                    Dim strValue As Object = ""
                    Dim Name As String = myarray(x)
                    oReg.GetStringValue(HKEY_CLASSES_ROOT,        TreeView1.SelectedNode.FullPath,
Name, strValue)
                    DataGridView1.Rows.Add()
                    DataGridView1.Rows(y).Cells(0).Value = Name
                    DataGridView1.Rows(y).Cells(1).Value = "REG_EXPAND_SZ"
                    DataGridView1.Rows(y).Cells(2).Value = strValue.ToString()
                    y = y + 1

                Case 7

                    Dim Name As String = myarray(x)
```

```vb
            Dim vls As Object = Nothing
            Dim Ve As Object = Nothing
            oReg.GetMultiStringValue(HKEY_CLASSES_ROOT,
TreeView1.SelectedNode.FullPath, Name, vls)
            Dim vl As Object
            For Each vl In vls
              If Ve <> "" Then
                Ve = Ve & ", "
              End If
              Ve = Ve + vl
            Next

            DataGridView1.Rows.Add()
            DataGridView1.Rows(y).Cells(0).Value = Name
            DataGridView1.Rows(y).Cells(1).Value = "REG_MULTI_SZ"
            DataGridView1.Rows(y).Cells(2).Value = Ve
            y = y + 1


        Case 4

            Dim Name As String = myarray(x)
            Dim dwValue As Object
            oReg.GetDWordValue(HKEY_CLASSES_ROOT,         TreeView1.SelectedNode.FullPath,
Name, dwValue)
            DataGridView1.Rows.Add()
            DataGridView1.Rows(y).Cells(0).Value = Name
            DataGridView1.Rows(y).Cells(1).Value = "REG_DWORD"
            Dim hexval As String = "0x00" + dwValue.ToString().PadLeft(6, "0") + " (" & dwValue
& ")"
            DataGridView1.Rows(y).Cells(2).Value = hexval
            y = y + 1


        Case 11

            Dim qwValue As Object
            Dim Name As String = myarray(x)
            oReg.GetQWordValue(HKEY_CLASSES_ROOT,         TreeView1.SelectedNode.FullPath,
Name, qwValue)
            DataGridView1.Rows.Add()
            DataGridView1.Rows(y).Cells(0).Value = Name
            DataGridView1.Rows(y).Cells(1).Value = "REG_QWORD"
```

```vb
                    Dim hexval As String = "0x00" + qwValue.ToString().PadLeft(6, "0") + " (" & qwValue
& ")"

                    DataGridView1.Rows(y).Cells(2).Value = hexval
                    y = y + 1

                Case 3

                    Dim value As String = ""
                    Dim strValue As Object = ""
                    Dim Name As String = myarray(x)
                    oReg.GetBinaryValue(HKEY_CLASSES_ROOT,        TreeView1.SelectedNode.FullPath,
Name, strValue)
                    DataGridView1.Rows.Add()
                    DataGridView1.Rows(y).Cells(0).Value = Name
                    DataGridView1.Rows(y).Cells(1).Value = "REG_BINARY"

                    For j = LBound(strValue) To UBound(strValue)
                      If value <> "" Then
                        value = value & ", "
                      End If
                      value = value + strValue
                    Next
                    DataGridView1.Rows(y).Cells(2).Value = value
                    y = y + 1

              End Select

          Next

      Case "HKEY_CURRENT_CONFIG"

          y = 0


          Dim inparams As SWbemObject = oReg.Methods_.Item("EnumValues").InParameters
          Dim outparams As SWbemObject = oReg.Methods_.Item("EnumValues").OutParameters
          inparams.hDefKey = HKEY_CURRENT_CONFIG
          inparams.sSubkeyName = TreeView1.SelectedNode.FullPath
          outparams = oReg.ExecMethod_("EnumValues", inparams)
          myarray = outparams.Properties_.Item("sNames").Value
          myTypes = outparams.Properties_.Item("Types").Value


          If IsDBNull(myTypes) = True Then
```

```vbnet
        Try

            Dim strValue As Object = ""
            oReg.GetStringValue(HKEY_CURRENT_CONFIG, TreeView1.SelectedNode.FullPath, "",
strValue)
            DataGridView1.Rows.Add()
            DataGridView1.Rows(y).Cells(0).Value = "(Default)"
            DataGridView1.Rows(y).Cells(1).Value = "REG_SZ"
            DataGridView1.Rows(y).Cells(2).Value = strValue
            y = y + 1
        Catch


        End Try

        Exit Sub

    End If

    For x As Integer = 0 To UBound(myTypes)

        Select Case myTypes(x)

            Case 1

                Dim strValue As Object = ""
                Dim Name As String = myarray(x)
                oReg.GetStringValue(HKEY_CURRENT_CONFIG,    TreeView1.SelectedNode.FullPath,
Name, strValue)
                DataGridView1.Rows.Add()
                DataGridView1.Rows(y).Cells(0).Value = Name
                DataGridView1.Rows(y).Cells(1).Value = "REG_SZ"
                DataGridView1.Rows(y).Cells(2).Value = strValue.ToString()
                y = y + 1

            Case 2

                Dim strValue As Object = ""
                Dim Name As String = myarray(x)
                oReg.GetStringValue(HKEY_CURRENT_CONFIG,    TreeView1.SelectedNode.FullPath,
Name, strValue)
                DataGridView1.Rows.Add()
                DataGridView1.Rows(y).Cells(0).Value = Name
```

```vbnet
                DataGridView1.Rows(y).Cells(1).Value = "REG_EXPAND_SZ"
                DataGridView1.Rows(y).Cells(2).Value = strValue.ToString()
                y = y + 1


            Case 7

                Dim Name As String = myarray(x)
                Dim vls As Object = Nothing
                Dim Ve As Object = Nothing
                oReg.GetMultiStringValue(HKEY_CURRENT_CONFIG,
TreeView1.SelectedNode.FullPath, Name, vls)
                Dim vl As Object
                For Each vl In vls
                    If Ve <> "" Then
                        Ve = Ve & ", "
                    End If
                    Ve = Ve + vl
                Next

                DataGridView1.Rows.Add()
                DataGridView1.Rows(y).Cells(0).Value = Name
                DataGridView1.Rows(y).Cells(1).Value = "REG_MULTI_SZ"
                DataGridView1.Rows(y).Cells(2).Value = Ve
                y = y + 1


            Case 4

                Dim Name As String = myarray(x)
                Dim dwValue As Object
                oReg.GetDWordValue(HKEY_CURRENT_CONFIG,   TreeView1.SelectedNode.FullPath,
Name, dwValue)
                DataGridView1.Rows.Add()
                DataGridView1.Rows(y).Cells(0).Value = Name
                DataGridView1.Rows(y).Cells(1).Value = "REG_DWORD"
                Dim hexval As String = "0x00" + dwValue.ToString().PadLeft(6, "0") + " (" & dwValue
& ")"
                DataGridView1.Rows(y).Cells(2).Value = hexval
                y = y + 1


            Case 11

                Dim qwValue As Object
```

```vbnet
                  Dim Name As String = myarray(x)
                  oReg.GetQWordValue(HKEY_CURRENT_CONFIG,  TreeView1.SelectedNode.FullPath,
Name, qwValue)
                  DataGridView1.Rows.Add()
                  DataGridView1.Rows(y).Cells(0).Value = Name
                  DataGridView1.Rows(y).Cells(1).Value = "REG_QWORD"
                  Dim hexval As String = "0x00" + qwValue.ToString().PadLeft(6, "0") + " (" & qwValue
& ")"
                  DataGridView1.Rows(y).Cells(2).Value = hexval
                  y = y + 1

            Case 3

                  Dim value As String = ""
                  Dim strValue As Object = ""
                  Dim Name As String = myarray(x)
                  oReg.GetBinaryValue(HKEY_CURRENT_CONFIG,  TreeView1.SelectedNode.FullPath,
Name, strValue)
                  DataGridView1.Rows.Add()
                  DataGridView1.Rows(y).Cells(0).Value = Name
                  DataGridView1.Rows(y).Cells(1).Value = "REG_BINARY"

                  For j = LBound(strValue) To UBound(strValue)
                    If value <> "" Then
                      value = value & ", "
                    End If
                    value = value + strValue
                  Next
                  DataGridView1.Rows(y).Cells(2).Value = value
                  y = y + 1

            End Select

          Next

      Case "HKEY_CURRENT_USER"

          y = 0


          Dim inparams As SWbemObject = oReg.Methods_.Item("EnumValues").InParameters
          Dim outparams As SWbemObject = oReg.Methods_.Item("EnumValues").OutParameters
          inparams.hDefKey = HKEY_CURRENT_USER
          inparams.sSubkeyName = TreeView1.SelectedNode.FullPath
```

```vbnet
            outparams = oReg.ExecMethod_("EnumValues", inparams)
            myarray = outparams.Properties_.Item("sNames").Value
            myTypes = outparams.Properties_.Item("Types").Value


            If IsDBNull(myTypes) = True Then

                Try

                    Dim strValue As Object = ""
                    oReg.GetStringValue(HKEY_CURRENT_USER,  TreeView1.SelectedNode.FullPath,  "",
        strValue)
                    DataGridView1.Rows.Add()
                    DataGridView1.Rows(y).Cells(0).Value = "(Default)"
                    DataGridView1.Rows(y).Cells(1).Value = "REG_SZ"
                    DataGridView1.Rows(y).Cells(2).Value = strValue
                    y = y + 1
                Catch


                End Try

                Exit Sub

            End If

            For x As Integer = 0 To UBound(myTypes)

                Select Case myTypes(x)

                    Case 1

                        Dim strValue As Object = ""
                        Dim Name As String = myarray(x)
                        oReg.GetStringValue(HKEY_CURRENT_USER,         TreeView1.SelectedNode.FullPath,
        Name, strValue)
                        DataGridView1.Rows.Add()
                        DataGridView1.Rows(y).Cells(0).Value = Name
                        DataGridView1.Rows(y).Cells(1).Value = "REG_SZ"
                        DataGridView1.Rows(y).Cells(2).Value = strValue.ToString()
                        y = y + 1

                    Case 2
```

```vbnet
            Dim strValue As Object = ""
            Dim Name As String = myarray(x)
            oReg.GetStringValue(HKEY_CURRENT_USER,        TreeView1.SelectedNode.FullPath,
Name, strValue)
            DataGridView1.Rows.Add()
            DataGridView1.Rows(y).Cells(0).Value = Name
            DataGridView1.Rows(y).Cells(1).Value = "REG_EXPAND_SZ"
            DataGridView1.Rows(y).Cells(2).Value = strValue.ToString()
            y = y + 1


        Case 7

            Dim Name As String = myarray(x)
            Dim vls As Object = Nothing
            Dim Ve As Object = Nothing
            oReg.GetMultiStringValue(HKEY_CURRENT_USER,
TreeView1.SelectedNode.FullPath, Name, vls)
            Dim vl As Object
            For Each vl In vls
              If Ve <> "" Then
                Ve = Ve & ", "
              End If
              Ve = Ve + vl
            Next

            DataGridView1.Rows.Add()
            DataGridView1.Rows(y).Cells(0).Value = Name
            DataGridView1.Rows(y).Cells(1).Value = "REG_MULTI_SZ"
            DataGridView1.Rows(y).Cells(2).Value = Ve
            y = y + 1



        Case 4

            Dim Name As String = myarray(x)
            Dim dwValue As Object
            oReg.GetDWordValue(HKEY_CURRENT_USER,        TreeView1.SelectedNode.FullPath,
Name, dwValue)
            DataGridView1.Rows.Add()
            DataGridView1.Rows(y).Cells(0).Value = Name
            DataGridView1.Rows(y).Cells(1).Value = "REG_DWORD"
            Dim hexval As String = "0x00" + dwValue.ToString().PadLeft(6, "0") + " (" & dwValue
& ")"
            DataGridView1.Rows(y).Cells(2).Value = hexval
```

```vb
                y = y + 1


        Case 11

            Dim qwValue As Object
            Dim Name As String = myarray(x)
            oReg.GetQWordValue(HKEY_CURRENT_USER,          TreeView1.SelectedNode.FullPath,
Name, qwValue)
            DataGridView1.Rows.Add()
            DataGridView1.Rows(y).Cells(0).Value = Name
            DataGridView1.Rows(y).Cells(1).Value = "REG_QWORD"
            Dim hexval As String = "0x00" + qwValue.ToString().PadLeft(6, "0") + " (" & qwValue
& ")"
            DataGridView1.Rows(y).Cells(2).Value = hexval
            y = y + 1

        Case 3

            Dim value As String = ""
            Dim strValue As Object = ""
            Dim Name As String = myarray(x)
            oReg.GetBinaryValue(HKEY_CURRENT_USER,          TreeView1.SelectedNode.FullPath,
Name, strValue)
            DataGridView1.Rows.Add()
            DataGridView1.Rows(y).Cells(0).Value = Name
            DataGridView1.Rows(y).Cells(1).Value = "REG_BINARY"

            For j = LBound(strValue) To UBound(strValue)
              If value <> "" Then
                value = value & ", "
              End If
              value = value + strValue
            Next
            DataGridView1.Rows(y).Cells(2).Value = value
            y = y + 1

        End Select

    Next


    Case "HKEY_LOCAL_MACHINE"
```

```vbnet
        y = 0

        Dim inparams As SWbemObject = oReg.Methods_.Item("EnumValues").InParameters
        Dim outparams As SWbemObject = oReg.Methods_.Item("EnumValues").OutParameters
        inparams.hDefKey = HKEY_LOCAL_MACHINE
        inparams.sSubkeyName = TreeView1.SelectedNode.FullPath
        outparams = oReg.ExecMethod_("EnumValues", inparams)
        myarray = outparams.Properties_.Item("sNames").Value
        myTypes = outparams.Properties_.Item("Types").Value


        If IsDBNull(myTypes) = True Then

            Try

                Dim strValue As Object = ""
                oReg.GetStringValue(HKEY_LOCAL_MACHINE, TreeView1.SelectedNode.FullPath, "",
strValue)
                DataGridView1.Rows.Add()
                DataGridView1.Rows(y).Cells(0).Value = "(Default)"
                DataGridView1.Rows(y).Cells(1).Value = "REG_SZ"
                DataGridView1.Rows(y).Cells(2).Value = strValue
                y = y + 1
            Catch



            End Try

            Exit Sub

        End If

        For x As Integer = 0 To UBound(myTypes)

            Select Case myTypes(x)

                Case 1

                    Dim strValue As Object = ""
                    Dim Name As String = myarray(x)
                    oReg.GetStringValue(HKEY_LOCAL_MACHINE,     TreeView1.SelectedNode.FullPath,
Name, strValue)
                    DataGridView1.Rows.Add()
                    DataGridView1.Rows(y).Cells(0).Value = Name
```

```
                    DataGridView1.Rows(y).Cells(1).Value = "REG_SZ"
                    DataGridView1.Rows(y).Cells(2).Value = strValue.ToString()
                    y = y + 1


            Case 2

                    Dim strValue As Object = ""
                    Dim Name As String = myarray(x)
                    oReg.GetStringValue(HKEY_LOCAL_MACHINE,         TreeView1.SelectedNode.FullPath,
            Name, strValue)
                    DataGridView1.Rows.Add()
                    DataGridView1.Rows(y).Cells(0).Value = Name
                    DataGridView1.Rows(y).Cells(1).Value = "REG_EXPAND_SZ"
                    DataGridView1.Rows(y).Cells(2).Value = strValue.ToString()
                    y = y + 1


            Case 7

                    Dim Name As String = myarray(x)
                    Dim vls As Object = Nothing
                    Dim Ve As Object = Nothing
                    oReg.GetMultiStringValue(HKEY_LOCAL_MACHINE,
            TreeView1.SelectedNode.FullPath, Name, vls)
                    Dim vl As Object
                    For Each vl In vls
                      If Ve <> "" Then
                        Ve = Ve & ", "
                      End If
                      Ve = Ve + vl
                    Next

                    DataGridView1.Rows.Add()
                    DataGridView1.Rows(y).Cells(0).Value = Name
                    DataGridView1.Rows(y).Cells(1).Value = "REG_MULTI_SZ"
                    DataGridView1.Rows(y).Cells(2).Value = Ve
                    y = y + 1


            Case 4

                    Dim Name As String = myarray(x)
                    Dim dwValue As Object
                    oReg.GetDWordValue(HKEY_LOCAL_MACHINE,       TreeView1.SelectedNode.FullPath,
            Name, dwValue)
```

```vb
            DataGridView1.Rows.Add()
            DataGridView1.Rows(y).Cells(0).Value = Name
            DataGridView1.Rows(y).Cells(1).Value = "REG_DWORD"
            Dim hexval As String = "0x00" + dwValue.ToString().PadLeft(6, "0") + " (" & dwValue
& ")"

            DataGridView1.Rows(y).Cells(2).Value = hexval
            y = y + 1


        Case 11

            Dim qwValue As Object
            Dim Name As String = myarray(x)
            oReg.GetQWordValue(HKEY_LOCAL_MACHINE,      TreeView1.SelectedNode.FullPath,
Name, qwValue)
            DataGridView1.Rows.Add()
            DataGridView1.Rows(y).Cells(0).Value = Name
            DataGridView1.Rows(y).Cells(1).Value = "REG_QWORD"
            Dim hexval As String = "0x00" + qwValue.ToString().PadLeft(6, "0") + " (" & qwValue
& ")"

            DataGridView1.Rows(y).Cells(2).Value = hexval
            y = y + 1

        Case 3

            Dim value As String = ""
            Dim strValue() As Object
            Dim Name As String = myarray(x)
            oReg.GetBinaryValue(HKEY_LOCAL_MACHINE,      TreeView1.SelectedNode.FullPath,
Name, strValue)
            DataGridView1.Rows.Add()
            DataGridView1.Rows(y).Cells(0).Value = Name
            DataGridView1.Rows(y).Cells(1).Value = "REG_BINARY"

            For j = LBound(strValue) To UBound(strValue)
              If value <> "" Then
                value = value & ", "
              End If
              value = value + strValue(j).ToString()
            Next
            DataGridView1.Rows(y).Cells(2).Value = value
            y = y + 1

    End Select
```

```
        Next

    Case "HKEY_USERS"

        y = 0

        Dim inparams As SWbemObject = oReg.Methods_.Item("EnumValues").InParameters
        Dim outparams As SWbemObject = oReg.Methods_.Item("EnumValues").OutParameters
        inparams.hDefKey = HKEY_USERS
        inparams.sSubkeyName = TreeView1.SelectedNode.FullPath
        outparams = oReg.ExecMethod_("EnumValues", inparams)
        myarray = outparams.Properties_.Item("sNames").Value
        myTypes = outparams.Properties_.Item("Types").Value


        If IsDBNull(myTypes) = True Then

            Try

                Dim strValue As Object = ""
                oReg.GetStringValue(HKEY_USERS, TreeView1.SelectedNode.FullPath, "", strValue)
                DataGridView1.Rows.Add()
                DataGridView1.Rows(y).Cells(0).Value = "(Default)"
                DataGridView1.Rows(y).Cells(1).Value = "REG_SZ"
                DataGridView1.Rows(y).Cells(2).Value = strValue
                y = y + 1
            Catch


            End Try

            Exit Sub

        End If

        For x As Integer = 0 To UBound(myTypes)

            Select Case myTypes(x)

                Case 1

                    Dim strValue As Object = ""
                    Dim Name As String = myarray(x)
```

```vbnet
                oReg.GetStringValue(HKEY_USERS,        TreeView1.SelectedNode.FullPath,      Name,
strValue)

                DataGridView1.Rows.Add()
                DataGridView1.Rows(y).Cells(0).Value = Name
                DataGridView1.Rows(y).Cells(1).Value = "REG_SZ"
                DataGridView1.Rows(y).Cells(2).Value = strValue.ToString()
                y = y + 1


            Case 2

                Dim strValue As Object = ""
                Dim Name As String = myarray(x)
                oReg.GetStringValue(HKEY_USERS,        TreeView1.SelectedNode.FullPath,      Name,
strValue)

                DataGridView1.Rows.Add()
                DataGridView1.Rows(y).Cells(0).Value = Name
                DataGridView1.Rows(y).Cells(1).Value = "REG_EXPAND_SZ"
                DataGridView1.Rows(y).Cells(2).Value = strValue.ToString()
                y = y + 1


            Case 7

                Dim Name As String = myarray(x)
                Dim vls As Object = Nothing
                Dim Ve As Object = Nothing
                oReg.GetMultiStringValue(HKEY_USERS,  TreeView1.SelectedNode.FullPath,  Name,
vls)

                Dim vl As Object
                For Each vl In vls
                  If Ve <> "" Then
                    Ve = Ve & ", "
                  End If
                  Ve = Ve + vl
                Next

                DataGridView1.Rows.Add()
                DataGridView1.Rows(y).Cells(0).Value = Name
                DataGridView1.Rows(y).Cells(1).Value = "REG_MULTI_SZ"
                DataGridView1.Rows(y).Cells(2).Value = Ve
                y = y + 1


            Case 4
```

```
                    Dim Name As String = myarray(x)
                    Dim dwValue As Object
                    oReg.GetDWordValue(HKEY_USERS,        TreeView1.SelectedNode.FullPath,      Name,
            dwValue)

                    DataGridView1.Rows.Add()
                    DataGridView1.Rows(y).Cells(0).Value = Name
                    DataGridView1.Rows(y).Cells(1).Value = "REG_DWORD"
                    Dim hexval As String = "0x00" + dwValue.ToString().PadLeft(6, "0") + " (" & dwValue
            & ")"

                    DataGridView1.Rows(y).Cells(2).Value = hexval
                    y = y + 1


            Case 11

                    Dim qwValue As Object
                    Dim Name As String = myarray(x)
                    oReg.GetQWordValue(HKEY_USERS,        TreeView1.SelectedNode.FullPath,      Name,
            qwValue)

                    DataGridView1.Rows.Add()
                    DataGridView1.Rows(y).Cells(0).Value = Name
                    DataGridView1.Rows(y).Cells(1).Value = "REG_QWORD"
                    Dim hexval As String = "0x00" + qwValue.ToString().PadLeft(6, "0") + " (" & qwValue
            & ")"

                    DataGridView1.Rows(y).Cells(2).Value = hexval
                    y = y + 1

            Case 3

                    Dim value As String = ""
                    Dim strValue As Object = ""
                    Dim Name As String = myarray(x)
                    oReg.GetBinaryValue(HKEY_USERS,        TreeView1.SelectedNode.FullPath,      Name,
            strValue)

                    DataGridView1.Rows.Add()
                    DataGridView1.Rows(y).Cells(0).Value = Name
                    DataGridView1.Rows(y).Cells(1).Value = "REG_BINARY"

                    For j = LBound(strValue) To UBound(strValue)
                      If value <> "" Then
                        value = value & ", "
                      End If
                      value = value + strValue
                    Next
```

```
                  DataGridView1.Rows(y).Cells(2).Value = value
                  y = y + 1

            End Select

      Next

      End Select

End Sub

End Class
```

Here's what the form looks like:

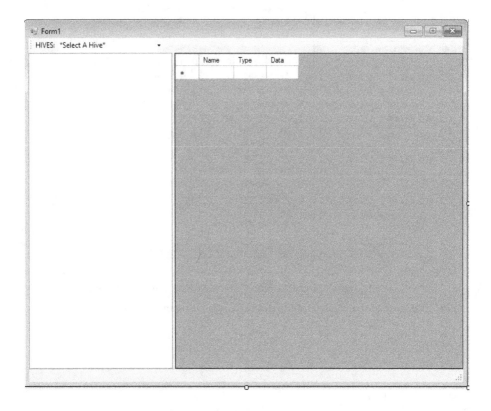

Real quick Explanation here. The Registry is broken down into "Hives" that is the first thing you select from the combobox. All of the folders that get you to where the

Names of the Values, types and Data are called subkeys. Which kind of rhymes with bees. (Apparently, the dev hated bees).

Anyway, once you find something that is useful – such as HKEY_LOCAL_MACHINE\System\CurrentControlSet\Control\Session Manager (Which is where you go if you want to know if your machine is pending a restart), your form should look like this:

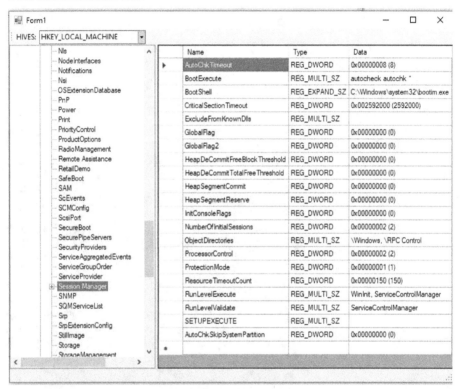

Click on the top of the DataGridView where is says name and the DataGridView will then organize the names in Alphabetical order as shown below:

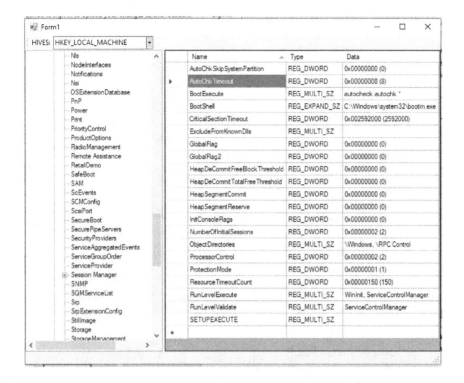

After adding a context menu to the project and adding it to the context menu in the DataGridView1 properties, add this code to the form with the DataGridView on it.

```
Private     Sub     ContextMenuStrip1_Opening(sender     As     Object,     e     As
System.ComponentModel.CancelEventArgs) Handles ContextMenuStrip1.Opening
    If DataGridView1.Rows.Count = 1 Then e.Cancel = True
End Sub

Private Sub CreateReportToolStripMenuItem_Click(sender As Object, e As EventArgs) Handles
CreateReportToolStripMenuItem.Click

    Dim ds As New System.Data.DataSet
    Dim dt As New System.Data.DataTable
    ds.Tables.Add(dt)
    classname = TreeView1.SelectedNode.Text

    Namesdic = New Dictionary(Of Integer, String)
    Widthdic = New Dictionary(Of Integer, String)
```

```vb
For x As Integer = 0 To DataGridView1.Columns.Count - 1
    ds.Tables(0).Columns.Add(DataGridView1.Columns(x).HeaderText)
    Namesdic.Add(x, DataGridView1.Columns(x).HeaderText)
    Dim d As Double = (DataGridView1.Rows(0).Cells(x).Size.Width * 0.7675)
    Widthdic.Add(x, d.ToString())
Next

For y = 0 To DataGridView1.Rows.Count - 1
    Dim dr As System.Data.DataRow = ds.Tables(0).NewRow
    For x As Integer = 0 To DataGridView1.Columns.Count - 1
        dr.Item(DataGridView1.Columns(x).HeaderText) = DataGridView1.Rows(y).Cells(x).Value
    Next
    ds.Tables(0).Rows.Add(dr)
Next

Create_The_Report(classname)

ds.WriteXml(Application.StartupPath & "\" & classname & ".xml")
ds.WriteXmlSchema(Application.StartupPath & "\" & classname & ".xsd")

Dim ds1 As New System.Data.DataSet

Dim myform As New Form2
myform.ReportViewer1.LocalReport.DataSources.Clear()
ds1.ReadXml(Application.StartupPath & "\" & classname & ".xml")
myform.ReportViewer1.LocalReport.ReportPath = Application.StartupPath & "\" & classname & ".rdlc"
myform.ReportViewer1.LocalReport.DataSources.Add(New Microsoft.Reporting.WinForms.ReportDataSource("DataSet1", ds.Tables(0)))
myform.ReportViewer1.RefreshReport()
myform.Visible = True

End Sub
```

When you're ready, run the code. When you click on create the report it will look exactly like what you are seeing in the DataGridView.

It will look like the image on the next page.

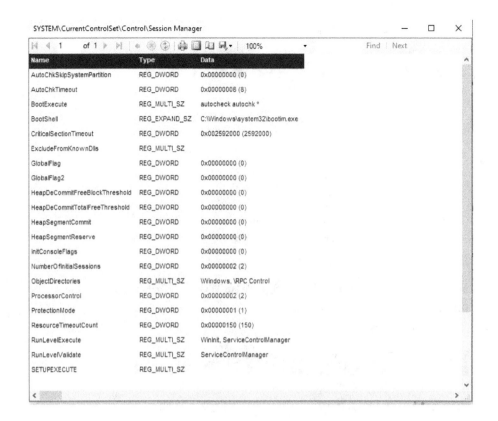

Name	Type	Data
AutoChkSkipSystemPartition	REG_DWORD	0x00000000 (0)
AutoChkTimeout	REG_DWORD	0x00000008 (8)
BootExecute	REG_MULTI_SZ	autocheck autochk *
BootShell	REG_EXPAND_SZ	C:\Windows\system32\bootim.exe
CriticalSectionTimeout	REG_DWORD	0x002592000 (2592000)
ExcludeFromKnownDlls	REG_MULTI_SZ	
GlobalFlag	REG_DWORD	0x00000000 (0)
GlobalFlag2	REG_DWORD	0x00000000 (0)
HeapDeCommitFreeBlockThreshold	REG_DWORD	0x00000000 (0)
HeapDeCommitTotalFreeThreshold	REG_DWORD	0x00000000 (0)
HeapSegmentCommit	REG_DWORD	0x00000000 (0)
HeapSegmentReserve	REG_DWORD	0x00000000 (0)
InitConsoleFlags	REG_DWORD	0x00000000 (0)
NumberOfInitialSessions	REG_DWORD	0x00000002 (2)
ObjectDirectories	REG_MULTI_SZ	\Windows, \RPC Control
ProcessorControl	REG_DWORD	0x00000002 (2)
ProtectionMode	REG_DWORD	0x00000001 (1)
ResourceTimeoutCount	REG_DWORD	0x00000150 (150)
RunLevelExecute	REG_MULTI_SZ	WinInit, ServiceControlManager
RunLevelValidate	REG_MULTI_SZ	ServiceControlManager
SETUPEXECUTE	REG_MULTI_SZ	

Creating these reports is so fast it is kind of addicting. Here's one from HKEY_CLASSES_ROOT\SOFTWARE\Microsoft\Windows NT\ CurrentVersion:

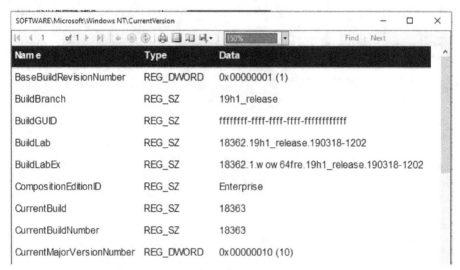

And another from HKEY_CLASSES_ROOT\SOFTWARE\ODBC\ODBCINST.INI\ODBC Drivers

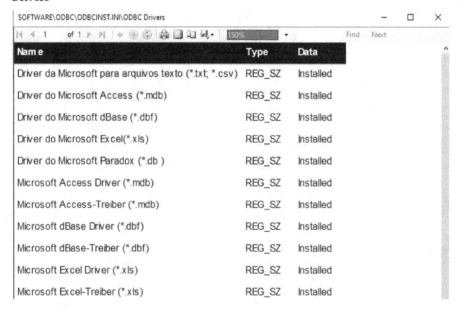

This program was running in x86 (32 bit) mode. How do I know? The number of entries and the types of drivers tells me it was.

After switching, so that the complier was running in I64(64bit) mode, going to the same location in the Registry, I recorded this:

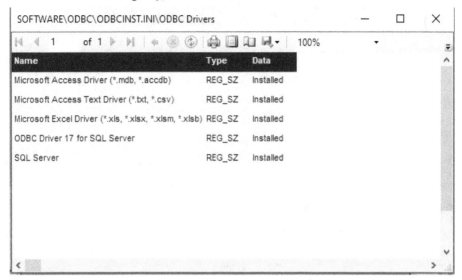

SOFTWARE\ODBC\ODBCINST.INI\ODBC Drivers

Name	Type	Data
Microsoft Access Driver (*.mdb, *.accdb)	REG_SZ	Installed
Microsoft Access Text Driver (*.txt, *.csv)	REG_SZ	Installed
Microsoft Excel Driver (*.xls, *.xlsx, *.xlsm, *.xlsb)	REG_SZ	Installed
ODBC Driver 17 for SQL Server	REG_SZ	Installed
SQL Server	REG_SZ	Installed

So, that should answer two questions.

One, can this code be used to make reports from the 64 bit registry without having to rewrite all the code?

Yes.

Two, are the two registries different enough to make reports from the two?

Yes.

You will find as I have over the many years of working with the registry that there is always something new and different to create interesting reports from. And, if you wanted to learn more about a specific subject involving IT, name me a better place to discover something new and different about your computer than on your computer itself.

How about Terminal Services?

Also, since we're taking less than 3 seconds to create one of these reports, what about the ability to see these reports with magnified print?

Name	Type	Data
Allow RemoteRPC	REG_DWORD	0x00000000 (0)
DelayConMgrTimeout	REG_DWORD	0x00000000 (0)
DeleteTempDirsOnExit	REG_DWORD	0x00000001 (1)
fDenyChildConnections	REG_DWORD	0x00000000 (0)
fDenyTSConnections	REG_DWORD	0x00000001 (1)
fSingleSessionPerUser	REG_DWORD	0x00000001 (1)
GlassSessionId	REG_DWORD	0x00000001 (1)
InstanceID	REG_SZ	3580bec7-75c6-4897-927c-2579473
NotificationTimeOut	REG_DWORD	0x00000000 (0)
PerSessionTempDir	REG_DWORD	0x00000000 (0)
ProductVersion	REG_SZ	5.1
RailShow allNotifyIcons	REG_DWORD	0x00000001 (1)
RCDependentServices	REG_MULTI_SZ	CertPropSvc, SessionEnv
RDPVGCInstalled	REG_DWORD	0x00000001 (1)
RDPVGSInstalled	REG_DWORD	0x00000001 (1)
SnapshotMonitors	REG_SZ	1
StartRCM	REG_DWORD	0x00000000 (0)
TSUserEnabled	REG_DWORD	0x00000000 (0)

Name	Type	Data
Callback	REG_DWORD	0x00000000 (0)
CallbackNumber	REG_SZ	
Domain	REG_SZ	
fInheritAutoLogon	REG_DWORD	0x00000001 (1)
fInheritCallback	REG_DWORD	0x00000000 (0)
fInheritCallbackNumber	REG_DWORD	0x00000000 (0)
fInheritInitialProgram	REG_DWORD	0x00000001 (1)
fInheritMaxDisconnectionTime	REG_DWORD	0x00000000 (0)
fInheritMaxIdleTime	REG_DWORD	0x00000000 (0)
fInheritMaxSessionTime	REG_DWORD	0x00000000 (0)
fInheritReconnectSame	REG_DWORD	0x00000000 (0)
fInheritResetBroken	REG_DWORD	0x00000000 (0)
fInheritShadow	REG_DWORD	0x00000000 (0)
fLogonDisabled	REG_DWORD	0x00000000 (0)
fPromptForPassword	REG_DWORD	0x00000000 (0)
fReconnectSame	REG_DWORD	0x00000000 (0)
fResetBroken	REG_DWORD	0x00000000 (0)
InitialProgram	REG_SZ	
KeyboardLayout	REG_DWORD	0x00000000 (0)
MaxConnectionTime	REG_DWORD	0x00000000 (0)
MaxDisconnectionTime	REG_DWORD	0x00000000 (0)
MaxIdleTime	REG_DWORD	0x00000000 (0)
NWLogonServer	REG_SZ	
Password	REG_SZ	
Shadow	REG_DWORD	0x00000001 (1)
UserName	REG_SZ	
WorkDirectory	REG_SZ	

  ❮ ▭   ❯

Also, things I find important is based on my own experiences with having to deal with the registry and, sometimes, what I find to be rather amusing. For example, DAO, as we were told back in the later 90s was being phased out.

Nice to see that DAO.DBEengine.120 is listed with the 64-bit registry entries.

I want to finish this book with some code that doesn't use the WMI StdRegProv.

In fact, it uses something much more powerful. I use this code to read both the 32-bit registry entries and the 64-bit registry entries. I just change the compiler settings and the report form's text so that the viewer knows which version is being displayed.

```
Imports Microsoft.Win32
Public Class Form3
    Private Sub Form3_Load(sender As Object, e As EventArgs) Handles MyBase.Load

    Dim x As Integer = 0
    Dim y As Integer = 0

    Dim Names() As String = Registry.ClassesRoot.OpenSubKey("Clsid").GetSubKeyNames
    For Each n As String In Names
      Dim regkey As RegistryKey = Registry.ClassesRoot.OpenSubKey("Clsid\" & n & "\Control")
      If IsNothing(regkey) = False Then
        DataGridView1.Rows.Add()
        regkey = Registry.ClassesRoot.OpenSubKey("Clsid\" & n & "\ProgId")
        If IsNothing(regkey) = False Then
          DataGridView1.Rows(y).Cells(0).Value = regkey.GetValue("")
        End If
        regkey = Registry.ClassesRoot.OpenSubKey("Clsid\" & n & "\VersionIndependentProgId")
        If IsNothing(regkey) = False Then
          DataGridView1.Rows(y).Cells(1).Value = regkey.GetValue("")
        End If
        DataGridView1.Rows(y).Cells(2).Value = n
        regkey = Registry.ClassesRoot.OpenSubKey("Clsid\" & n & "\InProcServer32")
        If IsNothing(regkey) = False Then
          DataGridView1.Rows(y).Cells(3).Value = regkey.GetValue("")
        Else
          regkey = Registry.ClassesRoot.OpenSubKey("Clsid\" & n & "\LocalServer32")
          If IsNothing(regkey) = False Then
            DataGridView1.Rows(y).Cells(3).Value = regkey.GetValue("")
          End If
        End If
      End If
      y = y + 1
```

```vb
            End If
        Next

    End Sub

    Private Sub CreateReportToolStripMenuItem_Click(sender As Object, e As EventArgs) Handles CreateReportToolStripMenuItem.Click

        Dim ds As New System.Data.DataSet
        Dim dt As New System.Data.DataTable
        ds.Tables.Add(dt)
        classname = "64bitControls"

        Namesdic = New Dictionary(Of Integer, String)
        Widthdic = New Dictionary(Of Integer, String)

        For x As Integer = 0 To DataGridView1.Columns.Count - 1
            ds.Tables(0).Columns.Add(DataGridView1.Columns(x).HeaderText)
            Namesdic.Add(x, DataGridView1.Columns(x).HeaderText)
            Dim d As Double = (DataGridView1.Rows(0).Cells(x).Size.Width * 0.7875)
            Widthdic.Add(x, d.ToString())
        Next

        For y = 0 To DataGridView1.Rows.Count - 1
            Dim dr As System.Data.DataRow = ds.Tables(0).NewRow
            For x As Integer = 0 To DataGridView1.Columns.Count - 1
                dr.Item(DataGridView1.Columns(x).HeaderText) = DataGridView1.Rows(y).Cells(x).Value
            Next
            ds.Tables(0).Rows.Add(dr)
        Next

        Create_The_Report(classname)

        ds.WriteXml(Application.StartupPath & "\" & classname & ".xml")
        ds.WriteXmlSchema(Application.StartupPath & "\" & classname & ".xsd")

        Dim ds1 As New System.Data.DataSet
        Dim myform As New Form2
        myform.Text = classname
        myform.ReportViewer1.LocalReport.DataSources.Clear()
        ds1.ReadXml(Application.StartupPath & "\" & classname & ".xml")
        myform.ReportViewer1.LocalReport.ReportPath = Application.StartupPath & "\" & classname & ".rdlc"
```

```vb
myform.ReportViewer1.LocalReport.DataSources.Add(New
Microsoft.Reporting.WinForms.ReportDataSource("DataSet1", ds.Tables(0)))
myform.ReportViewer1.RefreshReport()
myform.Visible = True


End Sub
End Class
```

Here's the 32-bit partial view:

ProgId	VersionIndependentProgId	ClassId	Location
		{64654B35-A024-4807-89D3-C6FDB5A260C7}	c:\Program File
		{A249E9F6-5B28-4ED1-8AF0-C9B9C5195486}	c:\Program File
		{2BA64696-55A2-4379-86E3-F2AD64FFEBA6}	C:\Program File
		{0CCFD0D9-36A6-46E7-982D-9E9DB4647BBA}	C:\Program File
AdobeAAMDetect.AdobeAAMDetect.2	AdobeAAMDetect.AdobeAAMDetect	{e8c77137-e224-5791-b6e9-ff0305797a13}	C:\Program File
AgControl.AgControl.3.0		{DFEAF541-F3E1-4c24-ACAC-99C30715084A}	C:\Program File
COMCTL.ImageListCtrl.1	COMCTL.ImageListCtrl	{58DA8D8F-9D6A-101B-AFC0-4210102A8DA7}	C:\Windows\S)
COMCTL.ListViewCtrl.1	COMCTL.ListViewCtrl	{58DA8D8A-9D6A-101B-AFC0-4210102A8DA7}	C:\Windows\S)
COMCTL.ProgCtrl.1	COMCTL.ProgCtrl	{0713E8D2-850A-101B-AFC0-4210102A8DA7}	C:\Windows\S)
COMCTL.SBarCtrl.1	COMCTL.SBarCtrl	{6B7E638F-850A-101B-AFC0-4210102A8DA7}	C:\Windows\S)
COMCTL.Slider.1	COMCTL.Slider	{373FF7F0-EB8B-11CD-8820-08002B2F4F5A}	C:\Windows\S)
COMCTL.TabStrip.1	COMCTL.TabStrip	{9ED94440-E5E8-101B-B9B5-444553540000}	C:\Windows\S)
COMCTL.Toolbar.1	COMCTL.Toolbar	{612A8624-0FB3-11CE-8747-524153480004}	C:\Windows\S)
COMCTL.TreeCtrl.1	COMCTL.TreeCtrl	{0713E8A2-850A-101B-AFC0-4210102A8DA7}	C:\Windows\S)

Here's the 64-bit partial view:

ProgId	VersionIndependentProgId	ClassId	Location
		{64654B35-A024-4807-89D3-C6FDB5A260C7}	c:\Program Files\
		{A249E9F6-5B28-4ED1-8AF0-C9B9C5195486}	c:\Program Files\
AdobeAAMDetect.AdobeAAMDetect.2	AdobeAAMDetect.AdobeAAMDetect	{e8c77137-e224-5791-b6e9-ff0305797a13}	C:\Program Files
CommunicatorMeetingJoinAx.JoinManager.2	CommunicatorMeetingJoinAx.JoinManager	{10336656-40D7-4530-BCC0-86CD3D77D25F}	C:\Program Files
Control.TaskSymbol.1	Control.TaskSymbol	{44F9A03B-A3EC-4F3B-9364-08E0007F21DF}	C:\Windows\sys
CTREEVIEW.CTreeViewCtrl.1		{CD6C7868-5864-11D0-ABF0-0020AF6B0B7A}	C:\Windows\sys
DOCSITE.DocSiteControl.1		{0006F024-0000-0000-C000-000000000046}	
FlashFactory.FlashFactory.1	FlashFactory.FlashFactory	{D27CDB70-AE8D-11cf-96B8-444553540000}	C:\Windows\Sys
Forms.CheckBox.1		{8BD21D40-EC42-11CE-9E0D-00AA006002F3}	C:\Program Files
Forms.ComboBox.1		{8BD21D30-EC42-11CE-9E0D-00AA006002F3}	C:\Program Files
Forms.CommandButton.1		{D7053240-CE69-11CD-A777-00DD01143C57}	C:\Program Files
Forms.Frame.1		{6E182020-F460-11CE-9BCD-00AA00608E01}	C:\Program Files
Forms.Image.1		{4C599241-6926-101B-9992-00000B65C8F9}	C:\Program Files
Forms.Label.1		{978C9E23-D4B0-11CE-BF2D-00AA003F40D0}	C:\Program Files

While I am pleased that I am able to create reports from both versions of the registry, I am totally shocked by what I see. C:\Window s.

Seriously?

I thought we allowed these people – Indian programmers have problems with American plurals – because there was a shortage of trained people here. But to change the word Windows to Window s in the Reports.

That is just plain arrogant and designed to make it harder for American Programmers to work with the APIs.

This is our country. Put it back to Windows. Screw with it in your country.

And, no, you won't see this mistake in Regedit. Nor do you see it in the Microsoft.Win32 API as shown below:

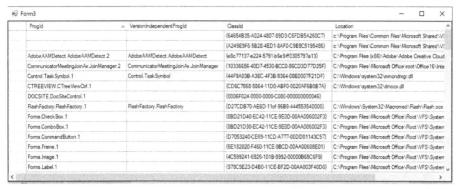

But you do see it in the report and what are we going to be showing our reports to? I also checked the XML:

```
—<Table1>
    <ProgID>Forms.CheckBox.1</ProgID>
    <ClassId>{8BD21D40-EC42-11CE-9E0D-00AA006002F3}</ClassId>
    <Location>C:\Windows\SysWOW64\FM20.DLL</Location>
  </Table1>
```

So, it is clearly not something we're doing in code. I will create a bug report and let Microsoft know about the issue.

With that said, it is time to finish this book and say goodbye for now.

Good luck with your career and stay safe!